THE AFRICA WE PRAY FOR
ON A PILGRIMAGE OF JUSTICE AND PEACE

Editors: Isabel Apawo Phiri and Collins Shava

THE AFRICA WE PRAY FOR
ON A PILGRIMAGE OF JUSTICE AND PEACE
Editors: Isabel Apawo Phiri and Collins Shava

Coordinator Editor WCC Publications: Lyn van Rooyen
Cover and book design: Michael Cagnoni
Web ISBN 978-2-88931-417-1
Print ISBN 978-2-88931-371-6

World Council of Churches	Globethics.net International
150 route de Ferney, P.O. Box 2100	Secretariat
1211 Geneva 2, Switzerland	150 route de Ferney
https://www.oikoumene.org	1211 Geneva 2, Switzerland
Email: publications@wcc-coe.org.	https://www.globethics.net
	Email: publications@globethics.net

CONTENTS

Foreword

It is my pleasure to congratulate the young people who took their valuable time to contribute to this publication on the Pilgrimage for Justice and Peace of the World Council of Churches (WCC). This publication is a result of an essay competition that involved important thematic areas of African society. The thematic areas of truth, trauma, displacement, gender justice and racial justice, among others, form some of the disturbing and sometimes contested issues in different countries.

This publication is also another indication of fruitful collaboration between the All Africa Conference of Churches (AACC) and WCC. Both institutions are on a pilgrimage, a common journey in our struggle for justice, peace, unity, and dignity of human life. One ecumenical family must work together tirelessly to make the world a better place.

The AACC is an ecumenical instrument of the churches in Africa with a continental presence in 43 countries. It has grown, and the Lord keeps transforming it to adapt to new needs and challenges in the continent. In our programmatic work, we endeavour to respond to the new and emerging issues in Africa and thus contribute to the transformation of Africa towards the realization of the continental dream, **Agenda 2063: The Africa We Want.**

At the centre and focus of our work are young people. We realize that young people are the present and the future leaders of our continent. Hence, we decided to dedicate this publication to harvest African stories sorely from our African youth.

Undoubtedly, the youth form the most significant demographic group on the continent. There is growing pressure for youth to succeed, leading to concomitant frustration. The continent has extremely limited jobs for young people, who find themselves also facing a myriad of contextual issues of conflict, instability, poor governance and oppressive regimes. These lead to unimaginable frustrations and hopelessness, making some of them risk their lives to migrate into even more hopeless situations.

Because of the hope we have in Africa, AACC supports a campaign for African patriotism under the motto: "Africa: My Home. My Future." We believe there is no better future for the African youth elsewhere than in Africa itself. It is important to rekindle the spirit of patriotism and encourage the youth to garner all their energy and resources to succeed in Africa. The youth need to be patriotic to their countries and Africa at large by utilizing their talents towards building a thriving continent.

This publication is an important contribution; the aspirations, hopes, and concerns of the youth in Africa, as they identify emerging issues from their contexts and suggest possible solutions to them. The churches must continue working with young people in this pilgrimage.

Rev. Dr Fidon R. Mwombeki

General Secretary, AACC

Foreword and Greetings

"The Africa We Pray for" – the title of this book reminds me of the Shona sculpture, which was a present of the Zimbabwe Council of Churches to the World Council of Churches (WCC) at the occasion of the 1998 WCC assembly in Harare. It stands today in front of the entrance to the conference hall of the Ecumenical Centre in Geneva, the home of the WCC secretariat. The statue of an African woman in prayer, turning her head towards God with closed eyes and obviously intensely listening interprets the theme of the assembly "Turn to God, Rejoice in Hope" in a unique way. The closed forms of her arms and legs remind the observer of a chain. In chains for many centuries, but unbroken, upright and listening to God in prayer, the sculpture is an image of the African continent with spiritual strength, full of hope, and thus with the power to liberate herself fully of the remnants of oppression, exploitation and slavery.

The WCC owes much to pioneers of African theology such as Mercy Amba Oduyoye and John Mbiti. Mercy Amba Oduyoye was youth education secretary of the WCC from 1967 to 1979. She served as deputy general secretary of the WCC from 1987 to 1994. Committed to strengthen women's voices, she became a founder of the Circle of Concerned African Women Theologians in 1989. John Mbiti was the director of the Bossey Ecumenical Institute from 1974 to 1980. This was the time when African and Black theology contributed significantly to the emerging contextual theologies whose leaders established in 1976 in Dar es Salam, Tanzania the Ecumenical Association of Third World Theologians (EATWOT). Mercy Amba Oduyoye became its first female president from 1997 to 2001. Both Oduyoye and Mbiti taught a new generation of African church leaders and of ecumenists from all over the world to appreciate the voices of faith from the African continent and to receive them as a gift to the people of Africa and indeed the one human family.

Isabel Apawo Phiri followed in the footsteps of Mercy Amba Oduyoye as general coordinator of the Circle of Concerned African Women Theologians and, since 2012, as deputy general secretary of the WCC. In a truly intergenerational approach, she is reaching out to younger theologians from the African continent and the diaspora, nurturing again a new generation of African scholars and ecumenists. Isabel Apawo Phiri and Collins Kudakwashe Shava, the youth executive secretary of the All Africa Conference of Churches

(AACC) in Nairobi, selected together impressive contributions of young African theologians for this volume. They address vital issues that affect the lives of youth from the ecological crisis to structural injustice, and the trauma of violence and war.

The PJP was envisaged by the 2013 WCC assembly in Busan, Republic of Korea. It translated the theme of the assembly "God of life, lead us to justice and peace" into action, strengthening the unity and common witness of churches together with all people of good will. Also, in 2013, the AACC held its own assembly coinciding with the fiftieth anniversary of the organization in Kampala, Uganda, with almost the same theme: "God of life, lead Africa to peace justice and dignity", emphasizing the dignity of all human beings who are made in the image of God as fundamental to the witness of the churches and their commitment to justice and peace. The close resonance of the two themes provided a solid ground for the common journey as pilgrims of justice and peace until today.

Isabel Apawo Phiri and Collins Kudakwashe Shava explain in their introduction why and how this book was produced. They offer this fruit of the close cooperation between AACC and WCC in the Pilgrimage of Justice and Peace (PJP) to the region and to the world so that the young people of Africa make themselves heard. May this book find readers who are ready to be moved and inspired by them.

I would like to take this opportunity to thank the general secretary of the AACC, Rev. Dr Fidon Mwombeki, wholeheartedly for his excellent cooperation with the WCC which is again visible in the joint production of this book. I also want to express my sincere gratitude to the two editors and all those who came before us in the journey of justice, peace and unity of the churches, humankind, and all creation.

Rev. Prof. Dr Ioan Sauca

WCC Acting General Secretary

Introduction:

The Africa We Pray for
on a Pilgrimage of Justice and Peace

Isabel Apawo Phiri and Collins Shava

Why the Book: The Pilgrimage of Justice and Peace

The World Council of Churches (WCC) assembly held in Busan in 2013 called on churches everywhere to walk together, to view their common life, their journey of faith, as a part of the Pilgrimage of Justice and Peace, and to join others in celebrating life and in concrete steps toward transforming injustices and violence. The invitation was to the WCC member churches, other Christians, people of other faiths and people of goodwill to walk, work and pray together. The WCC central committee meeting of 2014 further clarified the pilgrimage. They said:

> Declaring "We intend to move together" and inviting all people of goodwill to "join in pilgrimage", the delegates of the Busan assembly responded in a new way to the contemporary contextual challenges for the witness and very being of the churches, to the needs of people and creation yearning for justice and peace, and to the perceptions of many young people eager to see signs of hope.[1]

Through this document, it became clear that being on a Pilgrimage of Justice and Peace is: participating in God's mission towards life; moving to issues and places relevant for life and survival of people and the earth; deepening the fellowship of churches on the way with a strong spiritual dimension of common prayer and theological reflection; a journey of hope, looking for and celebrating signs of God's reign of justice and peace already here and now; and discovering opportunities for common witness and transformative action that make a difference in today's world with an open invitation to all people of goodwill.

---

1. *An Invitation to the Pilgrimage of Justice and Peace.* Document No. GEN 05. Central Committee 2-8 July 2014, Geneva, Switzerland.

The WCC central committee also recommended that, in our approach to the Pilgrimage of Justice and Peace, we should work with at least three different dimensions – not in a linear but much more in a dynamic, interdependent understanding: Celebrating the Gifts (via positiva), Visiting the Wounds (via negativa) and Transforming the Injustices (via transformativa). They also recommended that "as a seven-year programme emphasis, the pilgrimage will combine community-based initiatives and national and international advocacy for Just Peace, focusing on life-affirming economies; climate change; nonviolent peacebuilding and reconciliation and human dignity." As the different regions and churches engage with the themes, they should do so within their context, raising issues that are pertinent to them. Within the framework of the pilgrimage, in 2016, the central committee introduced the pilgrim team visits as one Pilgrimage of Justice and Peace methodology to show solidarity with one another. It was through analysis of the pilgrim team visits by the Reference Group on Pilgrimage of Justice and Peace and the Theological Study Group that new but related themes began to emerge. These lived experiences of the people visited are summarized in four themes: truth and trauma, land and development, gender justice and racial justice.[2] Therefore, this publication is Africa's lived experience of the pilgrimage from the perspective of young people.

Inspired by "The Africa We Want" Agenda

The African regional publication on the Pilgrimage of Justice and Peace is inspired by Agenda 2063: The Africa We Want.[3] This is the African Union's blueprint and master plan for transforming Africa into the global powerhouse of the future. The continent's strategic framework aims to deliver on its goal for inclusive and sustainable development and is a concrete manifestation of the pan-African drive for unity, self-determination, freedom, progress, and collective prosperity pursued under Pan-Africanism and African Renaissance. It came as a realization by African leaders that there was a need to refocus and reprioritize Africa's agenda from the struggle against apartheid and the attainment of political independence for the continent, which had been the focus of The Organization of African Unity (OAU), the precursor of the African Union. African leaders prioritize inclusive social and economic development, continental and regional integration, democratic governance,

---

2. The Ecumenical Pilgrimage of Justice and Peace– Towards an Ecumenical Theology of Companionship-A Study Document by the WCC-Reference Group and the Theological Study Group on the Pilgrimage of Justice and Peace.

3. Agenda 2063: The Africa We Want. https://au.int/en/agenda2063/overview.

peace, and security, amongst other issues, to reposition Africa to become a dominant player in the global arena[4].

With this background, the WCC and AACC initiated a process to collect youth voices on the Pilgrimage of Justice and Peace. The two organizations are eager to contribute towards the realizations of the Agenda 2063: The Africa We Want goals. Aspiration 6 of the African Union is an Africa whose development is people-driven, relying on the potential of African people, especially its women and youth, and caring for children. In this process, there was a deliberate move to include young people at the centre of the project. The essay competition provided a platform for youth to engage in research and write their aspirations of the Africa they want, an Africa they pray for, as they are the guardians of the future. The youth form the largest demographic group in Africa, which means the realizations of the Africa We Want goals rely on the active involvement of the youth. It is crucial for developmental partners contributing to the realization of Agenda 2063 to make a deliberate effort to ensure that young people are actively involved in decision making in all aspects of development, including social, economic, political, and environmental.

Young African men and women are the path-breakers of African knowledge. The creativity, energy and innovation of Africa's youth is the driving force behind the continent's political, social, cultural, and economic transformation. The essay competition explored the themes of truth and trauma, land and displacement, gender justice, racial justice that closely relate to the aspirations of the Agenda 2063 document. Young people creatively addressed these issues and provided recommendations for solving Africa's challenges.

Africa is a rising continent filled with numerous opportunities. The continent is endowed with abundant natural and human resources. However, it is battling a number of challenges that have limited its progress in the post-colonial era, as you may read in these essays from different contexts of the continent. You cannot miss the issues of unemployment, irregular migration, inequality, land disputes, gender-based and political violence, war, governance issues and failed political systems, which have given birth to highly contested and fraudulent elections in some parts of the continent. The youth, who form the demographic dividend, have grown up in an Africa with few opportunities for jobs. Some have known war and conflicts since birth, some have lived in hostile, oppressive regimes, and some are migrants who withstand the worst of xenophobia and racism. In all this, we see young

---

4. Agenda 2063: The Africa We Want: https://au.int/en/agenda2063/overview.

people of the continent who experience pressure to succeed in their countries and continent. It is no doubt that these issues can force young people to think that there are better opportunities to succeed outside Africa. They even risk drowning in the seas and taking chances with human traffickers just to be outside the continent.

It is these challenges that affect the progress of a continent that has abundant resources. The natural resources in the continent have been a source of conflict rather than of benefit to the people. Land grabs, displacement, physical and sexual violence, forced migration, and war have been associated with the presence of natural resources. The challenges date back to the colonial era in Africa. Post-colonial Africa is still working to make natural resources work for the people. Arguably, natural resources present an opportunity to change the continent's fortunes only if there are good institutions, policies, and human resources. It is quite interesting that in some of the essays, the youth managed to highlight this issue.

An Africa We Want, a continent we pray for, is also one that will give its people an opportunity to thrive and live a dignified life. To live in peace with dignity, the continent needs to confront the challenges it is facing. The continent must rise together with honest leadership, good governance, and strong democratic institutions. It must rise together with enhanced transparent and equal distribution of wealth and land. It must rise together with its human resources, who will be able to use their minds to harness the natural resources for the public. An Africa we pray for is one with men and women who have equal opportunities at all levels. The continent we pray for is one that must rise above these challenges for its people to live in dignity.

AACC Response: The Africa We Pray for

The general secretary of the All Africa Conference of Churches (AACC) at the General Assembly in Kigali in 2018, Rev. Dr Fidon Mwombeki, described AACC as an instrument of the churches in Africa, a strong ecumenical organization, with a continental presence and reach, an organization that grows and transforms itself to adapt to new needs of the churches in Africa. From 2018, the organization has led successful programs, including the Campaign for African Dignity, advocacy at the African Union, Agenda 2063, ecumenical theological education in Africa, gender justice and so forth.

The organization has continued to pursue new emerging themes, which the AACC 2018 General Assembly identified, particularly the challenge of migration and population explosion and a particular focus on the youth. In focusing on youth issues, the AACC has designed a campaign Africa: My Home, My Future, a campaign for Pan Africanism that seeks to inspire young people to be patriotic to their countries and Africa at large by utilizing their talents towards building a thriving continent. The campaign aims to create a generational movement made up of youth living in and outside the continent who are patriotic and have a passion for Africa. A movement that will steer conversations amongst young people of Africa on various issues that are affecting them.

Furthermore, AACC has created potent spaces for youth engagement and constructive conversations. The AACC has been driving a process to engage youth in various thematic areas, gender justice, peace, justice, climate, among many others. The essay competition on The Africa We Pray for, which has led to this publication, is one example of the platforms created. The process motivated the 2020 Pan African Youth Essay Competition on Extractives, Gender, and Inequality. This competition brought forward stories of young people living in resource-rich communities and those who have felt the effects of unequal distribution of wealth. Beyond youth work, the continental body remains a voice that campaigns for justice, peace, unity, and dignity. The AACC will continue to accompany the churches and countries in Africa to find solutions to continental challenges.

The Process of the Essay Competition

In July 2019, the WCC and AACC launched the call for essays themed The Africa We Pray for on a Pilgrimage of Justice and Peace.

Essays were to reflect on any of these four closely interrelated themes: Truth and Trauma (peacebuilding), Land and Displacement (economic, ecological justice and migration), Gender Justice, and Racial Justice.

The essays submitted were adjudicated on their contribution to the discussion on the Pilgrimage of Justice and Peace in the African context and how they examined the themes of the pilgrimage, with its three dimensions of celebrating life together, visiting wounds and engaging in transformative action. Authors were asked to submit texts of about 5,000 words, including notes and bibliography, with the condition that the scripts had not been published before or were under consideration for publication elsewhere. Essays were accepted in three official languages, English, French, and Portuguese.

By the submission deadline, the evaluation team had received thirty-two excellent essays. African staff of the WCC and the AACC reviewed all the submissions between October and December 2019. After a successful and rigorous adjudication process, twelve essays were selected to be in the Africa regional publication on the Pilgrimage of Justice and Peace, which will form part of the Pilgrimage of Justice and Peace regional harvests at the WCC 11th Assembly. Of the thirteen essays, six reflected on the theme of land and displacement, four on gender justice, and two on truth and trauma. However, there is clear evidence of an intersectional approach to the themes of the pilgrimage in most of the essays.

What Did We Learn from the Essays?

First, although we encouraged essays to cover any of the four closely interrelated Pilgrimage of Justice and Peace lived experience themes: Truth and Trauma (peacebuilding), Land and Displacement (economic, ecological justice and migration), Gender Justice, and Racial Justice, none of the shortlisted essays had a specific focus on racism. However, those articles with an intersectional approach touched on racism during the colonial period but not racism as experienced today. The reality of the African continent is that there is still experiences of racism where people from the global North are given priority over the local black people in private businesses, governments business contracts, standing in a queue in supermarkets, and, recently, who gets the COVID-19 vaccines first. Many cases are also shared in social media where the foreign-owned businesses in Africa do not treat their local workers well. South Africa is still struggling with the killing of farmers (both white and black). In addition, Africa continues to struggle with systemic racism and racial discrimination of minority ethnic groups and indigenous peoples. We conclude that on the Pilgrimage of Justice and Peace from the perspective of the youth, racism, racial discrimination, and xenophobia are significant issues in Africa, but it does not seem as pressing as truth and trauma, land and displacement, and gender justice.

The second lesson was on the difficulty of finding contributions from women. Very few submissions were received from women. Among the final twelve essays, only two were from women. Among those who wrote on gender justice, only one was a woman. On the one hand, it sent a positive signal that, among the youth, there are some men who have taken theological and biblical studies with a gendered perspective. For a very long time, studies from a women's perspective were very rare. The essays in this collection are an indication that there is some measure of success in promoting gendered perspectives.

On the other hand, it is concerning to see few women interested in making their voices heard through a competition because, since 1989, the Circle of African Women Theologians (hereafter the Circle)[5] have been mentoring young women to conduct research and publish on African issues from women's perspective. The Circle has generated various theological and biblical publications. It is not clear then why the young members of the Circle did not respond to the call for essays so that their perspective could be included in this publication. On the Pilgrimage of Justice and Peace, we see the need to strengthen girls and women's voices to share their experiences of the God of Life who leads us to justice and peace.

The third lesson relates to the reliance on the use of former colonial languages of English, French, Portuguese, and Spanish in order to communicate at continental level. This is because Africa has more than three thousand languages that go back to pre-colonial period. The invitation to the essay competition was sent out in English, French, and Portuguese. That meant that the African youth who cannot express themselves in writing in the three chosen colonial languages were excluded from the competition. In future we need to ask the churches to translate invitations to similar competitions in local languages and accept essays written in local languages too.

The majority of the essays received were in English. There were five essays in French, and no Portuguese essays were submitted. The ideal is that all final essays would be published in the three languages. Unfortunately, this is not financially viable at this stage. Hence the decision to include the two French articles in a predominantly English publication. Therefore, on the Pilgrimage of Justice and Peace, we acknowledge the many languages that we have inherited from our colonizers and hope that we can also write in our mother tongues.

Fourth, it is a deliberate decision of the WCC and AACC staff to prioritize the voices of the youth on the Pilgrimage of Justice and Peace in Africa in this publication. This is because we wanted to reflect the reality of the African demography. The United Nation Department of Economic and Social Affairs Division report on *Youth population trends and sustainable development* has the following information:

---

5. https://en.wikipedia.org/wiki/Circle_of_Concerned_African_Women_Theologians/.

'In Africa, the number of youth is growing rapidly. In 2015, 226 million youth aged 15-24 lived in Africa, accounting for 19 per cent of the global youth population. By 2030, it is projected that the number of youth in Africa will have increased by 42 per cent. Africa's youth population is expected to continue to grow throughout the remainder of the 21st century, more than doubling from current levels by 2055.'[6]

It is therefore essential to capture the perspective of the youth in Africa. Although the WCC considers people under thirty as youth, we extended the age limit for authors in this publication to thirty-five, as this is the age limit of the youth category in many WCC and AACC member churches.

Lastly, among the thirty-two essays received, a significant number came from the Catholic Church. Four of the final essays in this publication are from Roman Catholic authors. This is a testimony of the spirit of ecumenism in Africa, which goes beyond the membership of the WCC or AACC. It reflects the spirit of the invitation to the pilgrimage for WCC fellowship, other churches, people of other faiths, and people of goodwill to work together, walk together and pray together.

---

6. United Nations Department of Economic and Social Affairs. Population Facts No.2015/1 (2015) https://www.un.org/esa/socdev/documents/youth/fact-sheets/YouthPOP.pdf.

1

Economic and Ecological Justice
in the Zambian Context

Damon Mkandawire

Abstract

The current ecological and economic crises that are ruining planet Earth and impinging on its capacity to be a home for flora and fauna need to be addressed radically and immediately at all levels. Pollution, deforestation, land degradation, and poor sanitation, among other issues, threaten the health, harmony, and survival of all creation. This crisis provides an opportunity for reformation, renewal, restoration, and conversion in the church, which has a biblical injunction and mandate for environmental care, justice, and sustainability. This essay examines the role of the church in Zambia in promoting ecological and economic sustainability for the benefit of current and future generations. The author suggests that the church has the potential to have a positive impact on environmental care and sustainability and recommends that the church take the lead in bringing about ecological and economic justice.

Introduction

Zambia, like many African countries, is munificently blessed with productive soil and with precious natural resources that embody renewable resources (such as water, forestry, and fisheries) and non-renewable resources (minerals, coal, gas, and probably oil). These natural resources dictate the national economy and are central to the livelihoods of the majority of Zambians. Such resources represent financial gain and survival for most of Zambia's population, but the advantages accrued from the land and natural resources benefit only a few: the elite and mostly not the Zambians. Meanwhile, for those whose lands and waters are contaminated by mineral extraction, their only means of survival is subsistence farming or fishing or wage labour, which puts them in danger of exploitation. Natural resources represent a principal supply of public revenue and national wealth for some elites. In Zambia, natural resources can therefore be linked to poverty, slower economic growth, and, unfortunately, economic and ecological injustice.

Under normal circumstances, a natural resource boom can be an important catalyst for growth, development, and the transition from cottage industry to factory production. Indeed, with the right approach, natural resources can be used to transform a low-value economy that relies on exports of primary commodities to one with a substantial labour-intensive manufacturing base. The rich natural resource base for Zambia has instead brought about economic and ecological injustice, which can be referred to as "the resource curse."

Ecological and Economic Injustice in Zambia

The term "ecological justice" is often rendered as "eco-justice." The prefix "eco" comes from the Greek word for "house" (*oikos*) and is part of the etymological root of words like "economy" and "ecology," but also "ecumenism." Eco-justice challenges both humanity's destruction of the earth and the abuse of power which results in environmental damage, with poor people suffering the greatest impact.[1] Simply put, the concept of eco-justice entails that the value of non-human beings is not dependent on their usefulness to humans, and thus human beings have an obligation to take the inherent value of other living things into consideration whenever these living things are affected by human actions.

Economic justice is aimed at producing an opening for each person to have a dignified, productive, and creative life. Economic justice touches the individual person as well as the social order; it includes the moral principles which guide us in designing our economic institutions. These institutions determine how each person earns a living, enters into contracts, exchanges goods and services with others, and otherwise produces an independent material foundation for his or her economic sustenance.[2] The critical purpose of economic justice is to liberate each person to engage creatively in the unlimited work beyond earning a living: that of the mind and the spirit.

Ecological justice and economic justice are crucial to Zambian communities in the light of the enormous crisis of ecological destruction and poverty in the country. As such, a response is needed from ecclesiastical communities: providing a relevant theological perspective on ecological and economic justice that could assist in dealing with the crisis has become unavoidable.

---

1. Agbiji, O., 2015, 'Religion and ecological justice in Africa: Engaging "value for community" as praxis for ecological and socio-economic justice', *HTS Teologiese Studies/ Theological Studies* 71(2), Art. #2663, 10 pages.
2. Robin Hahnel, *Economic Justice and Democracy: From Competition to Cooperation* (London: Routledge, 2005), 15.

Extensive economic and technological activity has greatly enhanced global standards of living, especially in the developed world. African countries, including Zambia, have also benefited from these global economic and technological advances. Alongside these advances, environmental challenges have arisen: these are of such magnitude that the very existence of planet Earth is threatened. Global climate change, acid rain, the depletion of the ozone layer, rapid rates of deforestation, and significant increases in the rate of species lost suggest that the costs of global development are rising rapidly.[3]

Zambia and other parts of sub-Saharan Africa are experiencing the severe effects of environmental degradation arising from the extensive exploitation of copper and other minerals being carried out by multinational companies. For example, in Zambia – particularly in Mufulira District – the copper mined is processed through leaching or smelting. The smelting process produces sulphur dioxide gas (SO_2) and heavy metals. The SO_2 gas, which is acidic, has been the main source of air pollution.[4] Mining activities also have an effect on the soil quality around the site. During the beneficiation process, which extracts the more valuable minerals, some metal particles are transported by wind and deposited on the natural soil. This compromises the content of the soil and thus affects the growth of plants in the area. When SO_2 reacts with rainwater, a weak acid (acid rain) forms, which affects the soil's pH level and hinders vegetation growth. Acid rain also affects the iron roofing sheets of dwellings and the lives of animals. Leaks of hazardous materials, spills, and mine effluents have a bearing on the quality of the soil and stream water in which they are discharged.

Apart from multinationals bringing about environmental and economic injustice, two other challenges in the Zambian context further worsen the problem: poverty and poor governance/corruption. These two issues add to the pressure on natural resources and contribute to environmental degradation in Zambia. For example, the issue of high rates of deforestation can be attributed to poverty and poor governance or corruption. The facts speak for themselves. Zambia is ranked as one of the countries with the highest rates of deforestation in the world: this is estimated at around 1.5 percent per year.[5]

---

3. James H. Weaver, Michael T. Rock and Kenneth Kusterer, *Achieving Broad-based Sustainable Development: Governance, Environment, and Growth with Equity* (Sterling: Kumarian Press, 1997), 237.

4. ECZ. *Zambia Environmental Outlook Report 3.* Government printers. (2008).

5. Matieu Henry, Danai Maniatis, Vincent Gitz, David Huberman and Riccardo Valentini, "Implementation of REDD+ in Sub-Saharan Africa: State of Knowledge, Challenges and Opportunities," *Environment and Development Economics* 382-404: 4 (August 2011).

The leading factors of deforestation in Zambia are charcoal and wood fuel production, logging for timber, expansion of small-scale agriculture, and unsustainable agricultural practices.[6] Charcoal and wood fuel production (for domestic, commercial, and industrial uses) is a main driver of deforestation.

According to Power Africa, Zambia has 2,800 megawatts of installed electricity generation capacity, of which 85 percent is hydro-based. National access to electricity averages at 31 percent, with 67 percent of the urban population and 4 percent of the rural population having access to power. This fact brings to our attention the dependency of the majority of Zambians on charcoal.[7]

In the case of poverty, rural poor people are left with nothing but the natural environment; for many, poverty often forces them to hunt for game to be able to feed and care for their families. Unfortunately, their prey often include species that are facing extinction. In a typical rural environment in Zambia, raising issues of animal rights, game reserves, forest reserves, and endangered species not only sounds ridiculous; in fact, such issues hardly exist for rural people. For example, in some parts of Zambia, when there is a fish ban to allow the fish to breed and grow, the local poor fishermen do not understand the principle and will still go ahead and fish. Who can blame them? They have no other source of livelihood except the lake and fishing.

In the midst of all these resources in Zambia, the few elite continue to get richer while the poor continue to get poorer; their environment, which is their only source of livelihood, continues to be destroyed day by day. Who will speak for and with the poor and will also speak for the environment so we may have ecological and economic justice?

The Role of the Church in Ensuring Ecological and Economic Justice

We find ourselves at a time when we need a significant and credible theology of ecological and economic justice that is culturally relevant to Zambian communities. Developing such a theology could promote a purposeful ideological orientation for sustainable ecological and economic justice praxis.

---

6. Ministry of Lands and Natural Resources. National Investment Plan to Reduce Deforestation and Forest Degradation at https://climateinvestmentfunds.org/sites/default/files/meeting-documents/zambia_final_investment_plan_fip.pdf.

7. "Zambia: Power Africa Fact Sheet," US Aid, August 14, 2020, at: https://www.usaid.gov/powerafrica/zambia.

The modern environmental movement has encouraged a profound shift toward science, technology, and policy to solve large problems. Yet, environmentalists are increasingly aware that our current climate crisis will require more than just solutions based on hard science: these efforts must be accompanied by a widespread and deep-rooted change in individual norms and behaviour. Framing environmental action as a moral necessity is particularly important considering that many national and international agreements on climate change have stalled. The issue of ecological and economic injustice can create a platform for collaboration for diverse people and can bring the issues of poor people to the table. Fighting for people to live in a healthy environment is a moral and civil rights issue. Reconnecting all communities to nature and providing them with good reasons to be engaged is important.

To this effect, religious communities are well positioned to shape ecological and economic justice due to their influence over personal moral development. Africa's majority is religious. John Mbiti shared this unitary view of the pervasive religiosity of African traditional society. He wrote that Africans were reputed to be "notoriously religious" and asserted that they deserve this reputation, for they had traditionally been, and still are, "deeply religious," lived in "a religious universe," and possessed "a religious ontology."[8] He claimed that "religion permeates all the departments of life [in African societies] so fully that it is not easy or possible always to isolate it."[9] Moreover, he added, "religion is the strongest element in traditional background and exerts probably the greatest influence upon the thinking and living of the people concerned."[10] Africans, therefore, were religious beings: "it is this that makes Africans so religious: religion is in their whole system of being."[11]

Religion for an African, therefore, has a mandate for environmental care, justice, and sustainability. In the case of the Christian faith, the church's mandate can be drawn from a biblical text in Genesis 2:15, where the human is charged to take care of the garden or, simply put, the environment in which he or she was living. Kuzipa Nalwamba shares a similar thought when she says, "we cannot underestimate the power of sermons [religion]. The ... impact of churches in Zambia preaching ecologically sensitive sermons ... could make a difference and shape an ethos for earth keeping."[12]

---

8. John Mbiti, *Concepts of God in Africa* (London: SPCK, 1970).

9. Ibid.

10. Ibid.

11. Ibid.

12. Kuzipa Nalwamba, "'Spirited Bodies' as a Prerequisite for an Earth-keeping Ethos: A

The natural environment is the major domain and the source of livelihood for all human and non-human living things. It is from the environment that we get the fundamental prerequisite and essentials for life, such as air, water, food supplies, shelter, and clothing. Again, it is within the boundaries of the natural environment that we obtain medicinal supplies to treat the many sicknesses and diseases that have afflicted and plagued humankind over the years. The environment is also a source of employment in sectors such as agriculture, forestry, mining, quarrying, and fishing. The extent to which proper attention is given to the environment will determine its sustainability.

Throughout history, most religions or traditions in Zambia have traditionally expressed some ethical concerns for the environment and its creatures. Greed and destructiveness toward creation are condemned by most religious traditions. This view is reflected in their historical teachings, even if they are not put into practice. Traditionally, various cultures have highlighted ecological and economic justice. Proverbs, folktales, myths, legends, taboos, and ritual practices in Africa and in Zambia in particular focus on preserving and conserving the natural environment. There are rules and regulations on farming, fishing, hunting, the felling of trees, and sanitation. Stringent adherence to these traditional orders goes a long way in preserving some rivers, lagoons, trees, fish, and many other aspects of creation. Those who abuse them are sanctioned.

However, with the rise of modern society, these concerns have been fading. With the influx and development of modern science, economic and political institutions have taken the place historically accorded to religion, and traditional religious attitudes toward nature have largely disappeared. Yet, in other sectors, some religious leaders in Africa have returned to their origins to recover the pre-modern teachings to present them as religious environmental ethics. Perhaps it is time for the church in Zambia to join in the fight against environmental degradation. Jonathan Kangwa suggests that religion – in particular, Christianity – "plays a major role in shaping people's perceptions and attitudes. Especially the Bible as a sacred text may influence how people see the environment and the natural world."[13]

Juxtaposition of the First Creation Story of Genesis with Ubuntu Cosmogony," MA thesis, University of Pretoria, 2013, 194, https://repository.up.ac.za/bitstream/handle/2263/40334/ Nalwamba_Spirited_2013.pdf.

13. Jonathan Kangwa, "In Search of Indigenous Knowledge Systems for Ecological Justice: A Gendered Ecological Reading of Genesis 1–3 in the Context of the Tonga People of Zambia, PhD diss., University of KwaZulu-Natal, 2014, 18–23, http://researchspace.ukzn.ac.za/xmlui/ bitstream/handle/10413/12056/Kangwa_Jonathan_2014.pdf;sequence=1.

Jeremy Law, writing on Jürgen Moltmann's ecological hermeneutics, says that "For Moltmann … ecological crisis is to be found in neither the physical environment nor its social consequences. It is a crisis of values. It is a religious crisis."[14]

The biblical mandate of the church for environmental care is to commit to the task of promoting a sound and healthy environment, to care for people, the poor, the marginalized, wildlife species, and plants. It links environmental concerns with social justice issues. The two purposes of this care are for sustainable development and environmental integrity. According to Sapru,[15] sustainable development encompasses meeting the needs of the present without compromising the ability of future generation to meet their own needs. It fosters economic growth without sacrificing the natural resources of a given community. It ensures access to natural resources for future generations. Finally, it creates environmental integrity, economic prosperity, and community liveability. On the other hand, environmental integrity is the protection and improvement of the air, water, and land, which all living things depend on for their survival. It means not only avoiding harm to the natural environment but enhancing the environment through developmental decisions.

Ian Bradley, in his book *God Is Green: Christianity and the Environment*, opens chapter 5 with an interesting question: "Does Christianity offer distinctive insight into the proper relationship between human beings and the rest of creation?" He goes on to ask, "Do Christians indeed have a special contribution to make to the Green movement and the battle to preserve the natural environment from the many threats that are now facing it?"[16] To both these questions, the answer is a strong "yes." As part of the human race, Christians can do their part by consuming less energy, going in for organic gardening, recycling their waste, and embracing any other environmentally friendly practice to reduce their carbon footprint. In this essay, I argue that these individual lifestyle changes are just a first step. Christians must use their collective power as the organized church to bring about structural changes. Christians are thus called upon to live the change that they would want to see in this world.

14. Jeremy Law, "Jürgen Moltmann's Ecological Hermeneutics," in *Ecological Hermeneutics: Biblical, Historical and Theological Perspectives*, ed. David G. Horrell, Cherryl Hunt, Christopher Southgate and Francesca Stavrakopoulou (London: T & T Clark, 2010), 224.

15. R. K. Sapru, *Development Administration* (New Delhi: Sterling, 1994), 41–42.

16. Ian Bradley, *God Is Green: Christianity and the Environment* (London: Darton, Longman and Todd, 1990), 90.

In both the Old and the New Testaments, we have ample evidence of scripture pointing to the fact that numerous moral tenets, regulations, and laws are aimed at protecting the environment. They depict the fact that the natural environment is good and reflects God's glory.

Every call to save the environment is predicated on human action. Environmental disasters such as land degradation, pollution, and deforestation have serious implications for humanity and the ecosystem; thus, the church acts in response to reverse the situation that humanity inflicts on the created order. There is also a more realistic view that nature and humanity are imperfect, as they are marred by sin and subject to decay. The church, therefore, works on nature to maintain it. John Grim and Mary Evelyn Tucker share this view. They say that if religious educators promote a spirituality that ignores responsibility for the world, they are not promoting a Christian spirituality, as people cannot fulfil themselves spiritually unless they walk in harmony with the earth.[17] Again, one cannot be a true creature of the earth unless one reflects with one spirit and soul on the meaning, beauty, loveliness, and essentials of all creation.[18] In Bradley's words, "We stand together with nature as fellow sufferers in this world of pain and sorrow and we also stand together with God as co-operators in his plan to perfect and complete creation."[19]

Small numbers of individual Christians have always been involved in the environmental debate. Churches, however, have dragged their feet. This was recognized 48 years ago, when Dr Elfan Rees of the World Council of Churches addressed the 1972 United Nations Conference on the Human Environment in Stockholm:

> I admit, Mr. President, that the churches were slower than you were in realizing the terrible implication of this problem [environmental degradation]. You have awakened us, but in so doing you have lit a fire you cannot extinguish. We will follow you as long as you advance, we will spur you if you halt and we will take a vociferous lead if you turn back.[20]

---

17. John Grim and Mary Evelyn Tucker, *Ecology and Religion* (Washington: Island Press, 2014), 13–16.

18. Ibid.

19. Bradley, *God Is Green*, 91.

20. Ron Elsdon, *Greenhouse Theology: Biblical Perspectives on Caring for Creation* (London: Monarch, 1992), 34.

In light of Dr Rees' statement, one begins to ask if the church has truly been in the fight against environmental degradation. How involved is the church in advocating for ecological and economic justice today?

Kuzipa Nalwamba says, "That absence of the Christian voice' in regard to the eco-crisis the nation [Zambia] faces can be attributed to the fact that Zambian Christianity still espouses biblical anthropology that regards human beings to be at the pinnacle of creation."[21] Can this pilgrimage of justice help to correct the biblical anthropocentrism of humans? Or is the pilgrimage of peace and justice creating an eco-friendly world?

Conradie and Ayre state that churches are therefore called upon to get their own house in order before they can prescribe an environmental praxis, ethos, and spirituality to others.[22]

The involvement of the church in addressing issues of environmental sustainability is key. In many African countries, churches command a lot of respect in terms of the number of loyal adherents, regular meetings, moral leadership, and, at times, the financial capacity to help come up with mitigation measures. "On purely pragmatic and functional grounds, the role of the church in general and religion in particular, cannot be ignored in addressing issues such as poverty, HIV/AIDS, health care to the vulnerable, gender-based violence, food security or environmental sustainability."[23]

Kuzipa Nalwamba and Teddy Sakupapa propose that the church taking part in environmental sustainability is not an option. In quoting Paul Santmire, they say, a theology of nature that is biblical, Christological, and ecological will also be ecclesiological. It will be incarnate in the life of the Christian community.[24] In worship, the community of faith will form its identity and theological matrix from its spiritual and ethical praxis in the world; revisionist ecological ethics will be first and foremost communitarian and only secondarily principled and prescriptive.[25]

---

21. Nalwamba, "'Spirited Bodies.'"

22. Ernst M. Conradie and Clive W. Ayre, "Ecclesiology and Ecology in Ecumenical Perspective," in Clive Ayre and Ernst Conradie, eds, *The Church in God's Household: Protestant Perspectives on Ecclesiology and Ecology* (Pietermaritzburg: Cluster Publications, 2016), 5.

23. Ibid.

24. Kuzipa Nalwamba and Teddy Chalwe Sakupapa, "Ecology and Fellowship (Koinonia): A Community of Life," in Ayre and Conradie, eds, *The Church in God's Household*, 80.

25. Ibid.

The church's call to service must be directed toward the life-affirming substance of all God's creation. Kuzipa Nalwamba and Teddy Sakupapa[26] note that a damaged and exploited earth is an unjust world: it calls for the church's hope and action. Environmental degradation that has led to the suffering of creation itself, economic disparity, and climate-induced migrations of people and animals, among other effects, calls for a reassessment of the Christian community's self-understanding and ways of being. An over spiritualized expression of the Christian faith that ignores the physical world of nature and the false dichotomy often drawn between the spiritual and the temporal stand radically challenged.

In radically challenging economic and ecological injustice, the church must realize that these problems of economic and ecological injustice are closely related; realistic solutions must tackle both simultaneously. This means the church must be ready to speak far beyond paper recycling and lead-free petrol and work toward a major shift in the balance of economic power between rich and poor nations. The church must play its prophetic role in speaking truth to power and be able to speak for and with the poor. The poor contribute less to the damaging of the earth, and so the richer nations should be held responsible. Who is better positioned to speak for and with the poor than the church?

Conclusion

The church in Zambia is in a good position to bring about ecological and economic justice, owing to the fact that 96 percent of the population professes to be Christian. This is an opportunity for the churches, regardless of denomination, to instill the values and earth-keeping ethos in the masses that belong to the church. Behavioural change is assured when the church develops a theology that seeks to bring about justice. The church is a moral force with spiritual energy which can contribute to long-term solutions to our complex environmental issues. The ecological and economic problems must be dealt with, but not only because of the chilling prospects of environmental degradation on the horizon; the real motivation must be the quest for authentic worldwide solidarity inspired by the values of charity, justice, and the common good. Advocating for ecological and economic justice in this sense is a response to God's command to till and keep the land (see Gen. 2:15) that God has entrusted to humanity, and it must serve to reinforce the covenant between human beings and the environment – a covenant that should mirror God's creative love.

26. Ibid.

2

The Africa We Pray for
On A Pilgrimage of Peace and Justice:
The Case of the Lesotho Evangelical Church in Southern Africa

Malebona Makoetje

Abstract

This essay shares the story of the pilgrimage of justice and peace in Lesotho through the initiative of the Lesotho Evangelical Church in Southern Africa (LECSA). The World Council of Churches' four themes of the Pilgrimage of Justice and Peace are truth and trauma, land and displacement, gender justice, and racial justice. This essay falls under the theme of land and displacement. Within this theme, it traces issues of economic and ecological justice and migration as experienced in Lesotho. It then examines how LECSA has organized its annual pilgrimages of justice and peace and invited the whole nation of Lesotho and neighbouring churches to participate. This reflection on the issues in Lesotho sees them in the context of building blocks toward the Africa we want and the Africa we pray for on the pilgrimage of justice and peace.

Introduction

Any discussion on land and displacement in Africa must include the story of the colonialization of Africa by the powerful countries of the global North. In the 17th century, different groups of people arrived in Basutoland (now known as Lesotho). In the 19th century, King Moshoeshoe I united these groups; hence, he is famously known as the founder of the Basotho nation. Later, King Moshoeshoe, who was hungry for peace in his nation, invited three French missionaries (who were and still are referred to as white people) to his territory. They were famous for preaching the good gospel of peace among nations. This act opened up space for groups of migrant Dutch farmers to come to Basutoland. They were allowed to stay through the customary law.[1]

---

1. SAHO. "Lesotho" https://www.sahistory.org.za/place/lesotho.

Nevertheless, as time passed, white people began infiltrating the country. Despite the signed treaty of friendship, Voortrekkers (also referred to as white people) invaded the country and declared a separate land; this would become the Orange Free State. This led to a series of inconclusive territorial wars between Basotho and the Dutch. Coming to Basotho's rescue, the British intervened and helped Basotho to regain its independence from the Voortrekkers. This situation was an eyeopener for King Moshoeshoe. He realized that the future of Basotho would always be at risk unless they associated with the British. As a result, in 1862, he wrote a letter to the governor of the Cape, Sir Philip Wodehouse, suggesting an alliance between the two territories.[2] For this reason, Basotuland became a British protectorate.

In 1869, negotiations with the Voortrekkers were held regarding the boundaries. At this time, a large portion of King Moshoeshoe's territory was ceded to the Orange Free State, including places such as Ficksburg, Fouriesburg, Thaba 'Nchu, and Ladybrand. In 1871, Basutoland was annexed to the Cape Colony.[3] Fast forward to 1966, when Lesotho gained its independence from the British.

This is just one example of how white people ended up colonizing African countries. Hence the current cry of most Africans under the popular notion of "Bring back our land!" This is without a doubt one of the prime reasons why some countries are not at peace. They feel that the previous justice system failed them. As a result, they are crying out to the current legal system. They are fighting not only for their own justice but also for that of their fore parents. When vital councils such as the Truth and Reconciliation Council try to reconcile people who have had differences in the past, "Bring back our land" is one of the greatest challenges.

Even though, over the past 50 years, the African Union has focused on decolonization, political independence, and the struggle against Apartheid, it did not look too deeply into the effects of Apartheid in countries that had long been decolonized and free. Hence, countries like Lesotho are celebrating their independence but are still eager to get back what they lost during the Apartheid era. This shows that such issues must be included in Agenda 2063.4 Two birds will be beaten with one stone, as this will also respond to Aspiration 4: "A peaceful and secure Africa." The past may be forgiven, but

____

2. Ibid.

3. Ibid.

4. African Union Commission, *Agenda 2063: The Africa We Want*, 2015, https://au.int/en/agenda2063/overview.

it is not easily forgotten. To this day, Basotho are still crying and fighting for their land, which is a huge part of the Free State province in South Africa. Much can be achieved by discussion, as communication breaks down many barriers. It would be wise for the two countries, through their Truth and Reconciliation Councils, to sit down, talk, and discuss a way forward in regard to Basotho land which was captured by the white South Africans. The church can also take part in this through the Christian Council of Lesotho, as it is already involved in justice and peace projects in the country.

Current Land Disputes

A reality television programme, *Rea Ribolla*, broadcast on Lesotho Television (LTV), aims to explore problems in people's lives and come up with a solution, if possible. Normally, people on the programme ask for legal assistance or other solutions from people who are trained in that particular field, crying out for justice to take its course. Ninety-nine percent of the time, it is an individual, family, or community seeking legal intervention in regard to land issues, to the point that a number of people believe that this programme specializes in resolving land issues in Lesotho.

In a recent *Rea Ribolla* programme, aired on 10 September 2019, a family was seeking legal help because one woman from their family had kicked her disabled father out of the home. The woman was claiming that it was her late mother's land, and therefore the father was not welcome. She reinforced her actions by showing a lease written in her name. When the justice system intervened, they showed that it was illegal for the woman to make her father leave. There were two reasons for this decision: first, the site cannot be under a child's name while a parent is still alive – that can happen only when both parents are deceased. Second, a lease cannot be written under just one name but must contain two names; the daughter might have gotten the lease illegally. This is living proof that our justice system is also failing us. Unfortunately, these kinds of situations bring no peace to the nation.

In another land dispute that was broadcast recently, a man had bought a site (with a house already built on it) from another Mosotho woman. However, after he had made the full payment, he ran into trouble. Other people had moved into the house! They were the children of the woman who had sold him the house, who was nowhere to be found. This was a complex legal issue. First, this was a home for the children, and they had every right to be there in a safe home and be protected. Second, the man also had a right to be there, because the house, or rather the site, was also supposedly a home for his kids, who also had a right to a safe home. This case makes it clear that we Basotho are still not knowledgeable about our legal system concerning land issues. Many people are cheated over land due to their lack of knowledge. They are being deprived of justice and peace.

Knowledge is power. The government needs to educate the community on legal topics, especially those that involve land ownership. This can be achieved easily, as pressing issues like HIV and AIDS have laid a foundation for how to educate the nation at large. The same pattern can be followed, but this time around, people will learn about their land rights and responsibilities. The church can also educate their congregations on such topics. Civil servants also need to understand that no one is above the law. Proverbs 24:24 says, "Whoever says to the wicked, 'You are innocent', will be cursed by peoples, abhorred by nations." This reveals that an injustice is an injustice. They had better start treating the entire nation equally, not giving special treatment to who they know. Luckily, such an aspiration is already included in Agenda 2063: an aspiration of good governance, democracy, and respect for human rights, justice, and the rule of law.

Displacements

The execution of projects such as infrastructure, mines, and dams led to physical and economic displacement as well as potential significant impacts on the livelihoods and socio-economic status of the local population. This is problematic because only the country's interests are considered and respected – not those of the people. Most of the problems they experience are social ones. For example, the community treasures their initial homes, because they were homes to their forefathers; those places have sentimental connections for them. Also, they are heartbroken when the graves of their loved ones are destroyed. Moreover, people are normally placed where there is free land, not considering that they have come from fertile land. This is a huge problem when it comes to the production of food, leading to poverty. Furthermore, people are to be given stipends when they must make such sacrifices, but many complain that the stipends are not enough relative to what they were earning from their previous land. The government focuses its energy on the rich land, not the people.

For example, recent displacements were done at Polihali in the Mokhotlong district. Around October 2020, communities were contesting the land compensation rates, claiming that they were too low; they demanded market-based compensation for their land and assets. For instance, they said that land compensation rates were too low compared to the benefits they received from ploughing, grazing, sourcing firewood, and digging medicine from their ancestral land. They also complained that they were denied their communal compensation funds as well as grazing land which they were promised, over eight years ago, when construction was beginning. Furthermore, the promise was to offer the community a certain amount of money, but the authorities refused to give the people the money in cash. People had still not been paid for their affected properties. Finally, the people noted that the compensation was not discussed with them but just imposed on them.[5]

Chief Ts'epo Seiso, on behalf of the principal chief of Mokhotlong, Chief Mathealira Seeiso, pleaded with the Lesotho Highlands Development Authority (LHDA) to meet the communities halfway on the rates. LHDA offers one-off payment or one-off compensation paid in instalments for a period not exceeding 50 years. Community leaders recently noted that the 50-year compensation policy that LHDA offered their communities violated the provisions of the *Lesotho Land Act of 2010*, which prescribes 99-year rights to land ownership.[6]

Another project that took place is the construction of the Metolong Dam. Not all families who were affected by the construction were compensated, but a high percentage of them were.[7] Other households were not compensated immediately because of unresolved disputes over land. Fortunately, only a few families had to be relocated. Most people chose to be compensated with money, not land. The project required the permanent acquisition of land to build the dam and create the reservoir and other permanent infrastructure, such as roads and operating offices.[8] This project is vital to the country because through it, the government of Lesotho was able to meet Maseru's domestic and industrial water requirements up to the year 2020 and possibly beyond.[9] The positive side of this project is that water goes through treatment. The water sector plays an important role in Lesotho's economy because not only is the water used by Basotho, but it is also sold to South Africa. Nonetheless, lack of development of water resources like sanitation pipes, human-made dams, and taps in the lowlands make it very hard to transport or export

---

5. Centre for Investigative Journalism, 2018

6. Ibid.

7. M. Phakela, "Metolong Authority Compensates Displaced Villagers," *Lesotho Times,* 31 August 2018.

8. Ibid.

9. Ibid.

water from the highlands to the lowlands. On the other hand, the project has submerged farmlands and squandered economic resources of the community which initially occupied the land where the dam and its other infrastructure is built.

Gentrification – the renovation of houses and stores in deteriorated neighbourhoods by upper- or middle-income families or individuals – has also contributed to displacement issues. This improves property values but often displaces low-income families and small businesses. Over the years, gentrification has gone through different waves. Through this process, street vendors or small business owners were removed from certain areas, especially urban ones. This is not a fair system for those that are removed. In the Maseru district, small businesses in certain areas are removed so prestigious buildings can be built. This leads to small businesses clustering in one place, resulting in more competition and lower sales. This is an advantage to the country and its economy, as it means a more dignified city and more income from "rich" business owners.

Communication is key. Developments can benefit both the country and the community where construction takes place. However, the community needs to be treated with respect. Money does not solve everything. If the community were involved in the project from the beginning, people would feel respected and would be less likely to complain. They would feel that they had a say and were contributing to the growth of the economy through giving up their land. People have a right to voice their opinions. The church is always ready to intervene in such peace-building discussions. This may soon be a thing of the past, as Agenda 2063 aims to invent and put in place participatory development and local governance. Deuteronomy 16:19 says that those who become judges must be impartial when they make legal decisions, even if someone important is involved. The government and the community are equally important.

Ecological Justice

One of the land developments in Lesotho is the Letseng diamond mine. The community surrounding the area where the mine is situated complained about a number of issues. Among the many grievances was the blocked river sources and polluted water, seized pastures and diseases which residents say are a result of the mining operations.[10] Without a doubt, these complaints led

---

10. Ntina Ntsoaki Majara, *Land Degradation in Lesotho: A Synoptic Perspective* (Stellenbosch: University of Stellenbosch, 2005).

to major disturbances of the ecology of the land around the mine.

For instance, rivers are a habitat for a number of animals and plants; blocked river sources may lead to the deaths of these animals and plants. Polluted water results in disease and death for living things that consume that water. Seized pastures means fewer food sources for animals that depend on those pastures. This may also result in high competition for pastures which were not seized, and therefore reduced amounts of food, which may lead to hunger, starvation, or even death for animals. These situations bring up the issue of ecological injustice to the land of Lesotho. The Letseng diamond mine is not the only perpetrator of ecological injustice; other major construction projects in Lesotho have done the same. Endangered or vulnerable species are due to habitat loss, the result of Lesotho Highlands Water Project works, infrastructure clearing and construction, roadways, and noise.

Most of Basotho depends on farming for income for their families, especially households in the highlands. Luckily, Lesotho is blessed with fertile soil. Lesotho's biodiversity is very rich. There are a lot of mountainous areas, most of which are covered in various shrubs, trees, grasses, flowering plants; wild animals live there. As well, Lesotho is not a dry country; it has no deserts. It also has some wetlands.

However, there are threats to this biodiversity, which become a threat or a disadvantage to the entire Basotho nation. Unfortunately, such threats are mostly caused by humans. Population pressure forces settlement in marginal lands, resulting in overgrazing, severe soil erosion, and soil exhaustion. Most people of Basotho in the highlands and some in the lowlands are owners of domestic animals such as cattle and sheep. Livestock ownership has been used as a measure of wealth for a long time. Animal herders search for rich land for their animals to feed; eventually, the land is damaged and lacks the nutrients it originally possessed.

Human interference is the major threat, as people use the land for medicinal plants, tourism, and commercial interests. Unsustainable harvesting is one of the major environmental problems in Lesotho. The community overharvests plants until the land and its nutrients are depleted. Most Basotho, especially those in the highlands, believe in tradition and culture, and therefore believe in traditional healers. These traditional doctors are the ones who tend to exhaust plants, as they use them for medicinal purposes.

The community exploits plants and animals to attract tourists. For example, spiral aloe, which is found in the Maloti mountains, is a rare plant which can survive in very dry environments. It is threatened because it is used for both medicinal and commercial purposes. Commercially, it is used to produce petroleum jelly, called *lekhala*, and is vital to the economy of Lesotho. Vultures face possible extinction because of attacks by shepherds to protect their livestock; also, some people sell vulture feathers and feet. In summer, the country sometimes experiences extreme temperatures, which can lead to uncontrollable fires. These wildfires consume the plants and nutrients in their path, leading to shortages.

Water pollution is mostly due to industrialization. It is usually caused by a leak or the flow of fertilizers and pesticides from the fields. This disturbs the ecology in water bodies; animals in that water die. The chemicals also alter the composition of the topsoil, making the land more susceptible to harmful fungi species. Over time, the land is eroded. If that land is a habitat to living things, these organisms are forced to move to find another shelter. They may die if they cannot find a proper habitat, or they may end up competing with other similar organisms. This places some animals at greater risk of extinction. Pollutants also create dry conditions, making the land more prone to wildfires that kill the organisms living there.

Hosea 4:6 says, "My people are destroyed for lack of knowledge." Most Basotho men are not knowledgeable about the consequences of many of their practices, such as overgrazing. The government needs to be more aggressive in educating the nation about ecological justice. As Proverbs 21:15a (CEV) states, "When justice is done, good citizens are glad." Communities surrounding land that has been chosen for development have been gracious enough to give up their land. It is only fair for them to be treated with justice by the construction companies. What happens there as well as what is used and disposed of there must not negatively affect the community. When justice is done, the community will be glad as well.

Basotho have places called Maboelle. This is grazing land which is not open all year – it is open only at chosen times of the year, and that's when animal are allowed to graze. If animals are found grazing there at other times, they are taken into captivity. There are also botanical gardens in Lesotho, though not many, that help preserve and produce indigenous plant species. Forest reserves, nature reserves, and national parks assist in protecting species and improving the country's economy, as they are tourist attractions. For example, Ts'ehlanyane National Park is home to a rich diversity of animals and plant species. Bokong Nature Reserve contains a number of wetlands

Because Africa as whole does not want to be left behind, Agenda 2063's goal 7 focuses on the implementation of sustainable natural resource management, biodiversity conservation, genetic resources, and ecosystems.

Migration

In the absence of new jobs at home, Basotho believe that migration to different parts of the world for employment is justified. Most Basotho migrate to South Africa in search of greener pastures. Meanwhile, people who work locally claim that their salaries are too low; this is because the country is still developing. On top of that, because Lesotho's education system is not on par with South Africa's, the government normally sends post-secondary to study in other countries, especially South Africa. Small numbers of other people migrate to other parts of the Southern Africa Development Community, other areas of Africa, and abroad. This has been happening for decades now: even our forefathers went to South Africa in the 1900s to work in the mines. They were later joined by women, who went to work mostly as domestic workers.

Migrant labourers contributed greatly to the country's economy, as the money they sent home reduced poverty in their households. Lesotho is known for its agricultural practices. Land is Lesotho's asset. Funds from remittances were used to purchase agricultural inputs to improve subsistence farming. However, since the early 1990s, the number of migrant labourers, especially men, has drastically declined.[11] Due to *phongola*, where employers send workers home, many families, as well as the country in general, are experiencing poverty. Although there is land for farming, there is no money for agricultural inputs. Climate change is only making things worse.

Many unfortunate human-trafficking incidents have taken place concern-ing the migration of Basotho to South Africa. Numerous first-time emigrants are deceived by emigrants who have been in South Africa for a longer time. The latter make deals with South Africans who want to use people as tools to generate money by making them prostitutes and drug dealers. Women and children are frequent victims. This is just one example of the violence and discrimination facing women and girls, who truly need to be empowered to

---

11. Anna Rocchi and Pietro Del Sette, *Lesotho: Rural Development and Migration* (2016), http://www.centrosaluteglobale.eu/site/wp-content/uploads/2016/05/Migration-and-Rural-Development-in-Lesotho-PDF.pdf.

reach full gender equality. Fortuitously, Africa's Agenda 2063 includes this issue.

For example, a woman was recently invited to the radio station Harvest FM, on a show hosted by Puseletso Mphana, to share her traumatic human trafficking experience in South Africa. Apparently, she was lured by her cousin to go and work there, with the cousin saying that she had found a job for her already. There was no job; her cousin was trading her for money to some Indians in South Africa who use women as prostitutes for their own benefit. The women are kept captive in a dodgy building where men force themselves on them. These men pay the Indians, and those sexually abused women get nothing at all. They are just slaves.

Most Basotho migrate illegally to South Africa because getting a passport in Lesotho is difficult and tiring. Applying for a passport means standing in very long lines. It is rare for everyone in the line to be assisted that same day. Also, people must pay for a passport, and the wait to receive it is long. For these reasons, a lot of Basotho cross the border illegally.

Applying for a work permit is also a long process and costs money, so many people migrate to South Africa without legal documentation. People without work permits are allowed to be in South Africa for a month or less. This is practically impossible, because some places are very far from Lesotho, and transportation is costly. As a result, a number of Basotho reside in South Africa illegally. Furthermore, some Basotho who migrate never return home. In Lesotho, such people are called Makholoa. This leads to increased poverty in the country, as families back home are not taken care of. With occupations such as farming on land, they need money to start and sustain the work.

Migration also happens internally. Most of the people move to the lowlands for job opportunities. Also, most post-secondary institutions are in the lowlands; in fact, all universities are in the lowlands, and only a few technical colleges are found in the highlands. Therefore, jobs and schools are a pull factor to the lowlands, especially in the capital city, Maseru. Meanwhile, due to the construction (Letseng diamond mines) happening in the highlands, in the district of Mokhotlong, a number of people have migrated to Lets'eng. A new village has even emerged called Lets'eng village. This is where both employees of the mine and people who went there to provide services such as tuck shops and cafés lived at first. Unfortunately, a lot of illegal activities take place in this area, such as diamond smuggling, drug dealing, alcohol abuse, and prostitution.

The government of Lesotho, through the office of the Minister of Development Planning, Dr Aumane, recently held a job summit. It is hoped that this will increase the number of job opportunities in Lesotho. This would reduce the rate of migration, and at the same time, the nation will receive income which will sustain them in their everyday life as well as in farming. Moreover, the church has been holding prayer gatherings, especially youth leagues, where the theme has been job creation in Lesotho.

Above all, the answer will be carrying out Agenda 2063 under the first goal, "A high standard of living, quality of life and well-being of all citizens," as it focuses on income, jobs, and decent work. With this goal being implemented, migration will not be a major solution to economic problems, and citizens will earn enough to cover their basic needs. Also, their income will help to improve agriculture, which will be a response to Agenda 2063's goal number 3, "healthy and well-nourished citizens."

The Pilgrimage of Peace and Justice in Lesotho (Leeto La Thapelo)

Since 2012, the Lesotho Evangelical Church in Southern Africa (LECSA) has held an annual walk, *Leeto la Thapelo*, which is literally translated as "the journey of prayer." In 2015, this walk was extended, because the church wanted to take part in the walk of Peace and Justice, which is better known as the Pilgrimage of Justice and Peace. This is the tool the church uses to pray for all negative issues affecting the country. Thus, the country considers the pilgrimage to be the church's transformative action. As the Bible says, "…for God all things are possible" (Matt. 19:26). The pilgrimage has taken place every year since then.

They follow the same route each year because it signifies something. It is the route the first missionaries, the Paris Evangelical Missionary Society from France, used when they came to spread the word of God and teach the nation about peace. It is approximately 160 km from Modderpoort in South Africa to Morija, Lesotho, where the missionaries eventually established a mission station which is now known as LECSA. The walk takes five days. Along the way, they make stops where the missionaries also rested, meaning that these are important LECSA historic places. At the stops, they pray, sleep, eat, share the history, and prepare for the journey ahead. One such place is called Pholomong LECSA congregation; the literal translation of its name is "the rest place." Another stop is Thaba-Bosiu LECSA, where King Moshoeshoe resided. The missionaries came to this place first to report to the king when they arrived in Lesotho.

This pilgrimage is not only for LECSA members. The entire nation is invited. The aim of the re-enactment of this walk is to spread the word of God, reignite faith in Christians, fundraise for the church, and, above all, serve as an urgent request to politicians in Lesotho, regardless of political party, to reflect on and ponder the fact that by inviting the missionaries to Lesotho, King Moshoeshoe I was tired of the senseless and brutal murders due to constant wars among his people. The biggest purpose for the pilgrimage in Lesotho is to pray for justice and peace for the people of Lesotho as they journey together. In 2018, the Pilgrimage of Justice and Peace in Lesotho was graced by the presence of pilgrims from the Uniting Presbyterian Church in Southern Africa. Different presbyteries have also taken part in the pilgrimage. Recently, the Leribe Presbytery held the pilgrimage of Justice and Peace.

Conclusion

It is obvious that the thirst for justice and peace is not only for the church, but a cry for all. This further shows that the Pilgrimage of Justice and Peace is not only an annual church event but a course with a great purpose. Jesus says, "Where two or three are gathered in my name, I am there among them" (Matt. 18:20). This is a hunger for justice and peace – a cry for liberty for the land in terms of the economy and ecological justice and migration. Fortunately, Agenda 2063 seems to have almost all of Africa's pressing issues covered, with assistance from the church. Indeed, there is still hope for a better future for Lesotho and for Africa.

3

The Mission of the Church Regarding Migration:

An Opportunity for Ecumenism

Elie Sango Nyembo

Abstract

This essay analyzes sociologically and theologically the issue of migration in the context of the Democratic Republic of the Congo. At the same time, it shows the connection between poverty, wars, and migration. It also proposes the kenosis of Christ as a theological foundation of migration. The author reflects on migration not as a problem for societies, but as an opportunity for the churches to rediscover and live their identities. In other words, welcoming migrants and ministering to them in love and compassion is another way of imitating Christ and being church.

Introduction

The Second Vatican Council invited the Roman Catholic Church to read the signs of the times and interpret them in the light of the gospel.[1] In a globalized world, as newspaper headlines are dominated by the displacements of people, migration can be seen as the defining sign of the times.[2] Some people move voluntarily for work, education, and tourism, but most people are forced to leave their homes to go "to new territories"[3] when faced with serious threats to their lives. The annual Global Trends Report of the United Nations High Commissioner for Refugees (UNHCR) shows that nearly 70.8 million people were displaced at the end of 2018. The Democratic Republic of the Congo (DRC) is not exempt from this issue. The DRC is among the ten largest countries in the world with a great number of forced displaced people. This essay studies the issue of displacement of people (migration) using a comprehensive method which is both sociological and theological. The essay is composed of five parts. The first will analyze the reality and the causes of migration in Congo; the second and third will reflect on the biblical

---

1. Pope Paul VI, *Gaudium et Spes* (On the Church and the Modern World), 7 December 1965, 4.

2. T.G. Cruz, *Towards a Theology of Migration* (London: Palgrave Macmillan, 2014), ix.

3. D. T Irvin, "Migration and cities: Theological Reflections," in *Contemporary Issues of Migration and Theology*, ed. E. Padilla & P. Phan (New York: Palgrave Macmillan, 2013), 73-93.

and theological foundations of migration; and the fourth and fifth will reflect on what is being done and what could be done better in the life and mission of the Catholic Church.

Social Analysis of Congo

The word "migration," from Latin *migare*, refers to the movement – whether temporary or permanent, voluntary or forced – of individuals and groups of people crossing territorial boundaries.[4] Migrants are people "residing outside their country of origin."[5] In this essay, the word "migrant" refers to both refugees and internally displaced persons (IDPs). Cruz notes that migrants are often labelled as "forced" or "voluntary" migrants, depending on the motivation of their displacement.[6] Those who have been driven from home due to ongoing wars, persecution, and natural calamities are forced migrants. Those who move out of their free will are voluntary ones. What drives and motivates the displacement of Congolese away from their homes?

Material Poverty and the Political War Situation

Agenda 2063 of the African Union Commission[7] presents the hopes and aspirations of the people of Africa. Among these aspirations are found the eradication of poverty and the transformation of social and economic life of people (no. 9). These two elements will be attained through improving quality of life, job creation, and investments that are ecologically oriented. At the level of governance, African people aspire to have "a universal culture of good governance, democratic values, gender equality, respect for human rights, justice and the rule of law" (no. 27). Above all, as conflicts and wars have torn the continent apart, the people aspire to peace, which should be realized in 2020 with the silencing of all guns (no. 32). What does our context tell us?

International Monetary Fund (IMF) reports on the country show that the DRC "is a fragile state and one of the poorest countries in the world despite vast natural resources."[8] In 2014, the report indicated that 77 percent of the

---

4. Elaine Padilla and Peter Phan, eds, *Contemporary Issues of Migration and Theology* (New York: Palgrave Macmillan, 2013), 2.

5. Cruz, *Towards a Theology of Migration*, 1.

6. Ibid., 2.

7. African Union Commission, *Agenda 2063: The Africa We Want*, 2015, at: https://au.int/sites/default/files/documents/33126-doc-01_background_note.pdf.

8. International Monetary Fund (IMF), *Democratic Republic of Congo: IMF Country Report* no 19/285 (2019), 4.

population lived below the poverty line, meaning on less than one dollar a day. Poverty and unemployment were widespread. Hence, the country was ranked 178th out of 185 countries on the 2016 Human Development Index.[9] In certain villages and towns, one can hardly find good roads, hospitals, health infrastructure, or schools. The country has been experiencing its worst outbreak of Ebola,[10] which the World Health Organization (WHO) declared a public health emergency of international concern in July 2018.

What about political wars or conflicts? According to the IMF report, "the country has experienced episodes of violent conflicts since independence in 1960 and a full-scale war from 1997 to 2001."[11] These wars have caused serious humanitarian crises, with "over five million displaced people and widespread violence against civilians."[12] In the conflict zones, people are killed, women are raped, children are forced into military service, and real misery happens. The conflict situation affecting the country for years has had a negative impact on the people's wellbeing. As a result, as Bevans says, "many migrants and refugees are on the move because of violence in their home countries."[13] It is from this same perspective that many Congolese have resorted to both voluntary and involuntary migration. They tend to move to places where their lives could be improved, where they can have food on the table, a decent roof over their head, education for their children, and, if they are lucky, a house or a more comfortable life.[14]

Current Situation of Congolese Migration

As seen above, in the Congolese context, political, social, and economic conditions lead to the displacement of people. There are IDPs within the country and refugees to neighbouring countries and around the world. As for IDPs, the UNHCR report recognizes that about 4.5 million people have been displaced between 2018 and 2020 in the Kasai, Tanganyika, Ituri, and Kivu regions due to escalating violence.[15]

---

9. UN Development Programme, *Human Development Indices and Indicators: 2018 Statistical Update* (Geneva: UNDP, 2018), http://hdr.undp.org/sites/default/files/2018_summary_human_development_statistical_update_en.pdf.

10. IMF, *Democratic Republic of Congo*, 5.

11. Ibid., 4.

12. Ibid.

13. S.B. Bevans, "Migration and Mission: Pastoral challenges, Theological Insights," in *Contemporary Issues of Migration and Theology*, ed. E. Padilla & P. Phan (New York: Palgrave Macmillan, 2013), 157-177.

14. Cruz, *Towards a Theology of Migration*, 4.

15. UNHCR, "DR Congo Emergency" (n.d.), https://www.unhcr.org/dr-congo-emergency.html.

In addition, the UNHCR report explains that as of 31 August 2018, 811,299 Congolese refugees are being hosted in African countries.[16] A significant number of Congolese refugees live in Uganda, Tanzania, Rwanda, South Africa, Burundi, and Zambia. The statistics show that the majority of these refugees (55.6%) are children; of the adults, 50.1 percent are men and 49.9 percent are women.

It is thought that if the socio-economic situation of the country does not change, the number of IDPs and refugees will increase. This argument is in line with Cruz's logical conclusion that as long as there is poverty and income inequality, as long as the country is unable to provide adequate and secure standards of living for the people, migration will continue to happen.[17] However, it is useful to recognize the complexity and multidimensionality of migration. The DRC is not only a country of origin, but also one of both transition and destination of people. Many people from Burundi, Rwanda, the Central African Republic, and the Republic of South Sudan have found refuge in the DRC. Following Vatican II's invitation, unless we look at this issue, we are not doing theology. What does the Bible say about migration?

Biblical Foundation of Migration

According to Grau, migration is "something profoundly human."[18] Human beings have been on the move for thousands of years.[19] The Bible relates "a migratory lineage sanctioned,"[20] whereby God forcibly banished Adam and Eve from the garden (Gen. 3:23-24) and made them "migrant labourers."[21] Afterward, God reversed the "migration out of the garden"[22] with the call of Abraham to leave his home for the city of Ur and then go to Canaan (Gen. 11:31–12:6). Abraham became a "wandering Aramean" (Deut. 26:5), whom

Grau considers "a chief migrant of Genesis."[23] After him, Isaac, Jacob, and Joseph lived a nomadic life, pushed by "a search for economic means caused by

16. UNHCR, Regional Update-DRC Situation-August 2018. https://data2.unhcr.org/en/ documents/details https://data2.unhcr.org/en/documents/details/66046.

17. Cruz, *Towards a Theology of Migration*, x.

18. M. Grau, "Circumambulating Exodus-Migration-Conquest: A Theological Hermeneutics of Migratory Narrativity," in *Contemporary Issues of Migration and Theology*, ed. E. Padilla & P. Phan (New York: Palgrave Macmillan, 2013), 11-29.

19. Irvin 2014:6.

20. Padilla and Phan, *Contemporary Issues*, 62.

21. Grau 2013:22.

22. Irvin 2013:86.

23. Grau 2013:21.

a severe drought in search for food"[24] in Egypt. After Egypt, Israel lived as wanderers, refugees, and migrants in the desert for 40 years before entering the promised land.[25] During the times of Judges, Kings, and Prophets, the Bible also relates some histories of forced migrations, which took the form of "dispersion and deportation"[26] into exile; the prophets interpret this as "divine judgment" (Amos 6:8-14; Is. 8:1-22) and invite the people to repentance. In this sense, migration can be seen in a positive sense, as "a way of seeking a new and better life"[27] and coming back to God.

The New Testament begins with the movement of John the Baptist leaving his comfort zone for the wilderness (Luke 1:39). As well, the Matthean genealogy presents four foreign women in the lineage of Jesus: Tamar, Rahab, Ruth, and Bathsheba[28]; their foreignness and moral life did not prevent them from being part of Israel. The New Testament also emphasizes an unjust Roman decree that forced Mary and Joseph to leave their home for Bethlehem, where Jesus was born (Luke 2:1-7). Shortly after his birth, the Holy Family fled into Egypt seeking refuge (Matt. 2:13-14) and afterward established themselves in Nazareth. George describes Jesus Christ as "a wandering teacher"[29] who was without a permanent residence. Jesus himself left his home to spread the gospel in Galilee, travelling all over Judea. Eventually, he went to Jerusalem, where he encountered his death. What is Jesus' attitude toward migration?

In his encounter with the Samaritan woman, he broke the cultural barrier of conversing with women of doubtful reputation as a way of breaking down the barrier between Judeans and Samaritans (John 4:7-30). In his preaching, Jesus invites his listeners to practise *"xenophilia,"*[30] that is, to care for the stranger and those who are rejected, because they represent Christ (Matt. 25:35, 38, 43). This is what Pagán qualifies as "the sacramental presence of Christ."[31] In addition, the Acts of the Apostles situates

---

24. Ibid.

25. D. Field and J. Koslowski, eds., *Prospects and Challenges for the Ecumenical Movement in the 21st Century* (Geneva: Globethics.net, 2016), 75.

26. Ibid., 130.

27. D. Schoenfeld, "'You Will Seek from There': The Cycle of Exile and Return in Classical Jewish Theology," in *Theology of Migration in the Abrahamic Religions*, eds. E. Padilla & P. Phan (New York: Palgrave Macmillan, 2014) (27-45), 28.

28. Padilla and Phan, *Theology of Migration*, 77.

29. K.M. George, "Theology of Migration in the Orthodox Tradition," in *Theology of Migration in the Abrahamic Religions*, eds. E. Padilla & P. Phan (New York: Palgrave Macmillan, 2014) (27-45), 62-76.

30. Padilla and Phan, *Theology of Migration*, 77.

31. L. N. R. Pagán, "Xenophilia or Xenophobia: Toward a Theology of Migration," in

the foundation of the church in the "dispersal of the Greek-speaking disciples after the martyrdom of Stephen."[32] Stephen's speech in Acts 7 relates the migration history of the Patriarchs. It emphasizes that, as God is the God of the pilgrim people, the church should not be afraid of going to the ends of the earth. Irvin claims that "Christians were, for the first several centuries, without a homeland, without a place they could politically call their own."[33] This trend of ideas has guided missionary ventures in spreading the gospel to the ends of earth: from Jerusalem to the East (Antioch), from the East to the West (Rome), and from the West to the "New World".[34] In what sense does migration speak about God? What is the theological foundation of migration?

Kenosis: The Theological Foundation of Migration

To construct a theological reflection (from below) on migration, Daniel Groody suggests starting from the migrant's experiences. According to Groody, "migration helps to explain the kenosis of Jesus Christ."[35] He holds that "the spirituality of these migrants has more to do with self-emptying than self-fulfillment."[36]

Kenosis appears to be one of the oldest Christological statements in the Bible. From the Old Testament, Schonborn understands kenosis as "condescension" or God's "descent"[37] for the redemption of humanity. In his work of creation and redemption, God accepts to limit Godself, making Godself small and dwelling among people (*Shekinah*). The same notion is developed by the prophet Hosea, whereby God is intimately involved in human affairs; God "allows himself to be abused."[38] Phan talks about *"Deus migrator"*[39] and *"imago Dei migratoris."*[40] He stresses that God is the "Primordial Migrant"[41] who freely and out of love migrates from eternity and embraces humanity.

Contemporary Issues of Migration and Theology, ed. E. Padilla & P. Phan (New York: Palgrave Macmillan, 2013), 42.

32. Bevans 2013:157

33. Irvin 2014:13

34. Padilla and Phan, *Theology of Migration*, 78.

35. D.G. Groody, "The Spirituality of Migrants: Mapping an Inner Geography," in *Contemporary Issues of Migration and Theology*, ed. E. Padilla & P. Phan (New York: Palgrave Macmillan, 2013), 139-156.

36. Ibid., 147.

37. C. Schonborn, *God Sent His Son* (San Francisco: Ignatius Press, 2004), 113.

38. P.J. Colyer, *The Self-emptying God.* (Newcastle: Cambridge Scholars Publishing, 2013)

39. Padilla and Phan, *Theology of Migration,* 97.

40. Ibid., 99.

41. Ibid., 97.

The notion that God saves and cares for God's creation shaped the Christian understanding of the mystery of incarnation and the interpretations of the passion and death of Jesus Christ.

In the New Testament, Philippians 2:5-8 explains well the kenosis of Jesus Christ. In this passage, the movement of the Son of God in the economy of salvation is described as "a humiliation or emptying,"[42] taken from the Greek word *kenosis*. Kenosis refers to the emptying, lowering, and humility shown by Jesus Christ in the incarnation (v. 6), his taking on the worst human condition of slavery (v. 7), and his acceptance of the cross, with its consequences of death (v. 8). It is in this perspective that Courau[43] strongly affirms that in loving humankind totally, "Christ descended to the lowest level … until his agony." All this culminates in the divine love shown on the cross. Jesus manifested his kenosis (translated as "love") by dying for us. For this reason, Balthasar identifies the divine love as the purpose of "God's movement towards creation."[44] He argues that God is not, in the first place, "absolute power" but "absolute love."[45] Kenosis is the preferring of the other to oneself. The Father's love (kenosis) is expressed in God's preferring us to God's Son by handing him over for humanity's sake. In the same way, the Son prefers us to himself, to his own life, which he abandons for our benefit. The Spirit is continually described as "the gift of them both."[46] In other words, the Trinity holds nothing back to itself.

How does the kenosis of Christ relate to migration? Three considerations could be deduced from the above assumptions. First, in replacing the word "kenosis" with "migration," we find that we cannot talk about God without migration. As a result, creation becomes a crucial moment where

by God migrates and "encounters humanity."[47] Repeatedly, God lowers (migrates) Godself to conclude covenants with Israel, to communicate Godself with humanity, whatever their responses (Israel's infidelity). Phan insists that "the incarnation of God's Word in Jesus of Nazareth can equally be regarded

---

42. J.M. Carmody, "Kenosis," in *New Catholic Encyclopedia*, ed. Berard L. Marthaler, Thomas Carson and Joann Cerrito (Washington: Thomson Gale, 2003), 143.

43. "Pour aimer totalement l'homme, le Christ est descendu au plus bas, …, jusqu'à son agonie." T.M. Courau, "La dimension kénotique du dialogue," *Documents Episcopat* 10: 11 (2014), 50–55, at 52.

44. Hans Urs von Balthasar, *Theo-Logic: Theological Logical Theory: II: Truth of God*, trans. Adrian J. Walker (San Francisco: Ignatius Press, 2004), 327–28.

45. Hans Urs von Balthasar, *Mysterium Pascale*, trans. A. Nichols (Norwich: T&T Clark), 28.

46. Ibid.

47. K. Anatollis, *Athanasius* (London: Routledge, 2004), 42.

as God's migratory movement."[48] In the incarnation, Godself overcomes the distance between God-self and humanity. God bends down to reach humanity while raising humanity to Godself.[49] The encounter between God and humanity in Jesus Christ is extended to the cross and his death, which is "the extreme descent of the Word into our condition."[50]

Second, the kenotic itinerary (migration) taken by Christ from eternity into eternity could be understood in terms of a pilgrimage. Irvin stresses that "the Christian biblical witness ends with a grand pilgrimage, with the migration of the humankind up to and into the New Jerusalem."[51] He highlights that for both the living and the dead, the end is the migration into the New Jerusalem, because "the gates [of the New Jerusalem] will never be shut" (Rev. 21:25). Third, Cruz associates migration with salvation. She thinks that migrants move in order to live.[52] In their pilgrimage, like Christ, some encounter suffering, obstacles, unjust policies, and even death.[53] However, the author recognizes that Jesus' death was not the last word: there is "life that comes after death."[54] To this, Groody adds that "immigrants also relinquish everything they own, knowing that their one companion and lasting security is God and God alone."[55] How does the experience of migrants help us understand the kenosis of Christ?

In today's world of anti-immigrant sentiments, discourses, and policies, every migrant experiences a life that images the kenosis of Christ. Most migrants experience the feeling of humiliation, going down, becoming weak, and a descent to death, which were also in Christ. Groody elaborates: "even when they do not die physically, they undergo a death culturally,

psychologically, socially and emotionally."[56] These are daily realities lived by migrants: poverty, anxiety about the future, loss of national identity, and loss of personal dignity. Pagán says that "many migrants have become nobodies, disposable people, or wasted lives."[57] Illegal immigrants live in fear for their lives

---

48. Padilla and Phan, *Theology of Migration,* 99.

49. Anatollis, *Athanasius,* 33.

50. Ibid., 45.

51. Irvin 2014:86.

52. Cruz, *Towards a Theology of Migration,* 24.

53. Ibid., 23.

54. Ibid., 24.

55. Groody 2013:152.

56. Ibid., 149.

57. Pagán 2013:38.

and are at times affected by xenophobic attacks; tag names (stereotypes) are bestowed on them. Some migrants are killed, accused of organ trafficking[58] or selling drugs, and are used as scapegoats to justify the frustration caused by economic crises. Cruz accentuates that even when they are legal migrants, some people suffer from "the inequities in the education or health care system."[59] To this, we could add "wage discrimination"[60] and gender inequalities, especially for women, who may depend on male family members for access to health care in a patriarchal and sexist system.[61] In short, we will affirm that in his kenosis, Jesus Christ profoundly identifies with, shares, and struggles with migrants' conditions of alienation and discrimination[62] before, during, and after migration.

If God, who is almighty, operates in a kenotic way with all vulnerability, love, self-offering, and descent "into the lower parts of the earth,"[63] what about us? How do we respond to this situation as a church?

Ethical and Ecclesiological Responses to Migration

Ethical Responses

Philippians 2:5-8 determines our responses to migration. Our moral action should be about following and imitating Christ (v. 5). Christ's way of life should become our modus operandi. This is not an outward imitation but should touch our innermost being. Concretely, what should we do? Pagán reiterates the teaching of the Torah and invites us to care for the strangers.[64] We are invited to speak up for refugees and make space for them (Lev. 19:34). *Sollicitudo Rei Socialis* extends our actions to nations and calls for solidarity, that "the stronger and richer nations must have a sense of moral responsibility for the other nations."[65] Meanwhile, the US bishops' pastoral letter *Strangers No Longer: Together on the Journey of Hope* tells us that our common faith in Jesus Christ should move us to search for ways that favour a spirit of

---

58. In Zambia, in April 2016, Rwandan refugees and other foreign nationals were accused of ritual killings. N. Mwale and J. Chita, *The Church's Social Responsibility in Zambia: The Catholic Response to the 2017 Prejudiced Attacks on "Others"* (Lusaka: University of Zambia: 2017), 132–156, at 132.

59. Cruz, *Towards a Theology of Migration*, 6.

60. Ibid., 18.

61. Ibid., 33.

62. Ibid., 93.

63. H.U. Balthasar, *Who Is a Christian?* (San Francisco: Ignatius Press, 1994).

64. Pagán 2013:38.

65. Pope John Paul II, *Sollicitudo Rei Socialis* (30 December 1987), 39.

solidarity.[66] These ethical considerations invite us to rethink our ministry from the perspective of migration.

Ecclesiological Responses

The church's mission originates in Godself, who, out of God's love (kenosis) externalizes, migrates, journeys into our sinful and broken world, and communicates God's love manifestly in creation, in incarnation, and on the cross.[67] According to Bevans, "mission and migration have been closely intertwined since the earliest days of the Church."[68] In fulfilling her mission in a migration context, the church is called to "exist for men and not for herself."[69] Expounding from *Ad Gentes*, which says that "Christian charity truly extents to all,"[70] Rahner accentuates that Christians should serve everyone inclusively: the poor, the old, the sick, and all the people at the edge of society,[71] including migrants. Loving service and self-sacrifice for others are the attitudes celebrated in the Philippian hymn which the church should imitate and incorporate. Hospitality might be the best way of practising this option, which could be done by both individual institutions and ecumenically. Bevans thinks that, for instance, the church could offer "a temporary home to newly arrived migrants."[72] Manchala thinks that hospitality goes beyond "being polite to a guest, but it should be guided by compassion, good will and right relationship."[73] Another area to venture into is that of justice, peace, and the integrity of creation.[74] This means that the church should defend the rights of migrants and denounce any racist or xenophobic sentiment or legislation.

---

66. USCCB, *Strangers No Longer: Together on the Journey of Hope* (2003), 6, https://www.usccb. org/issues-and-action/human-life-and-dignity/immigration/strangers-no-longer-together-on-the-journey-of-hope.

67. Secretariat for Non-Christians, Dialogue and Proclamation, 1991, 9.

68. Bevans 2013:157.

69. Karl Rahner, *The Shape of the Church to Come*, trans. Edward Quinn (London: SPCK, 1974), 61.

70. *Ad Gentes* (On the Mission Activity of the Church), 7 December 1965, 12, http://www. vatican.va/archive/hist_councils/ii_vatican_council/documents/vat-ii_decree_19651207_ad-gentes_en.html.

71. Rahner, *The Shape of the Church to Come*, 62.

72. Bevans 2013:163.

73. D. Manchala, "Migration: An Opportunity for broader and deeper Ecumenism," in *Theology of Migration in the Abrahamic Religions*, eds. E. Padilla & P. Phan (New York: Palgrave Macmillan, 2014) 161.

74. Bevans 2013:165.

Susanna Snyder embraces the soteriological interpretation of the church and thinks that the church should not be thought of as serving immigrants but rather as "a migrant Church."[75] Cruz shares this view and calls for "a Church of the stranger."[76] It is in this perspective that Peter Phan adds to the Creed: "I believe in One, Holy, Catholic, Apostolic and Migrant Church."[77] A migrant church does not simply affirm otherness but seeks to be enriched with the differences. Liturgy is a way of living this option. For instance, one could include in liturgical celebrations prayers for migrants, prayers for governments to provide just laws for migrants, and prayers for particular groups of migrants in times of acute crisis or suffering. Embracing liturgical inculturation in a migrant church will reveal that there is not only one liturgy in the church. Another way of being a migrant church would be incorporating, in the life of the church, migrants' traditions, histories (personal, family, ecclesial), biases, and lived faith.[78]

The challenge that the migrant church presents is about making migrants full members of the church with equal rights, allowing them to share in the responsibilities, and up to, for instance, integrating their popular devotions in the liturgy.

We agree with Ratzinger that "there is no such thing as religion in the abstract."[79] This means that the solution to the issue of migration should be addressed concretely. Pope Francis, various congregations, and ecumenical bodies have begun showing how to live and minister to migrants kenotically.

Positives Elements of Our Times

Pope Francis

Since his inauguration on 3 March 2013, Pope Francis has called the Church to "go forth from our own comfort zone in order to reach all the 'peripheries' in need of the light of the Gospel."[80] He insists that pastors

75. Susanna Snyder, *Asylum-Seeking, Migration and Church* (London: Routledge, 2012), 4.

76. Cruz, *Towards a Theology of Migration*, 92.

77. Peter Phan, "Doing Ecclesiology in the World Church," lecture at the Oblate School of Theology, San Antonio, 17 October 2017, https://ost.edu/video-peter-phan-ecclesiology-world-church.

78. J. Vought and R. Barton, "Pilgrimage as Spiritual Communion," *Ecumenical Trends* (April 2012), 11–14, at 11.

79. Pope Benedict XVI, *In Communio, Vol. 1: The Unity of the Church* (Grand Rapids: Eerdmans, 2010), 148.

80. Pope Francis, *Evangelii Gaudium* (The Joy of the Gospel), 24 November 2013, 20, https://www.vatican.va/content/francesco/en/apost_exhortations/documents/papa-francesco_esortazione-ap_20131124_evangelii-gaudium.html.

should be operating more on the road and on a journey. This invitation moves the church from all forms of exclusivity and highlights "inclusivity and service."[81] The Pope articulates what he has at heart: "I prefer a Church which is bruised, hurting and dirty because it has been out on the streets, rather than a Church which is unhealthy from being confined and from clinging to its own security."[82] In his pastoral practices, the Pope has surprised many: for instance, he makes the Vatican closer to the people by "his radical inclusion of the homeless and the poor at the Vatican,"[83] the majority of whom are migrants. Again, while on a pastoral visit in the United States, for instance, the Pope shared meals "with the homeless rather than the elected power"[84] of the US Congress. The Pope's pastoral orientation shows that his core priority is that the church lead by example and "become a poor Church for the poor"[85] and a migrant church.

Religious Congregations

Apart from the Pope, different congregations within the Catholic Church work with and for the migrant as way of promoting justice, peace, and the integrity of creation. The religious congregations working with migrants provide "basic means and aids for integration,"[86] which consist of providing legal support (advocacy) and language courses for quick reinsertion. All this is done selflessly, without the intention of converting the migrants to the Catholic faith, but "in the dialogue of sincerity and love."[87]

Among many congregations are the Scalabrinians – priests who operate a network of migrants and provide spiritual, religious, and practical support for unauthorized migrants.[88] The Jesuit Refugee Service is also known for providing educational support to many African migrants. In addition, the Missionaries of Africa (White Fathers) support and minister to African migrants in strategic points in Africa (South Africa, Mali, and the Maghreb), in Europe (Germany), and in North America (Canada).[89] In their ministry,

81. G. Mannion, *Pope Francis and the Future of Catholicism* (New York: Cambridge University Press, 2017), 102.

82. Ibid., 49.

83. Ibid., 102.

84. Ibid.

85. Ibid., 97.

86. C. Stenschke, "Migration and Mission," *Missionalia* 44: 2 (2016), 129–51, at 147.

87. Pope Paul VI, Ecclesiam Suam, 6 August 1964, 112.

88. Cruz, *Towards a Theology of Migration*, 79.

89. The Missionaries of Africa have created the Africa Centre (Canada) and Afrika Center (Berlin) as places of awareness raising, encounter, and support for the African communities in

they promote African cultures through liturgical celebrations and other events. One notices what Cruz says, that "migrants bring with them a new sense of being a Church with all their devotions, novenas, day of the dead celebration, they also bring their own saints."[90] Liturgical inculturation in the context of migration "often brings about a reinvigorated Church in terms of worship and spirituality."[91] It is in this sense that the Congolese migration communities are known for having vibrant liturgical celebrations. Furthermore, in living in a globalized way, both the challenges and opportunities related to migration should not be handled by a single entity. Migration also demands "a joint effort and an ecumenical vision."[92] Padilla and Phan call for "an interdisciplinary approach"[93] toward migration, whereas Pagán calls for an international, ecumenical, and intercultural approach, because migration is an international problem.[94] It is in this sense that, *ad intra*, the Missionaries of Africa (men) and the Missionary Sisters of Our Lady of Africa (women) formed a mixed community working with migrants in Germany. Today, there is a need to broaden activities toward ecumenical outreach. No church can find solutions to migration alone. The right time, the *kairos*, to journey, to walk in solidarity with the migrants as churches is now.

Ecumenical Realizations: "Exchange of Gifts"

The experience of Christians travelling, learning, praying, and practising ecumenism in the social sphere is not new in many countries. In the words of Ratzinger, in the DRC, the Catholic Church has remained "the only trusted entity which functions and makes life continue, which provides the necessary assistance, and helps to find the possibility of creating one great solution."[95] For these reasons, the World Council of Churches invites the churches to "practise a culture of encounter, hospitality, and cordial welcome for migrants."[96] How is this call being lived?

---

partnership with migrant organizations: https://mafrome.org.

90. Cruz, *Towards a Theology of Migration*, 81.

91. Ibid.

92. D.O. Terfassa, "Migration and Inclusive Communities," in *Prospects and Challenges for the Ecumenical Movement in the 21st Century*, eds. D. Field, D & J. Koslowski (Geneva: Globethics. net, 2016) 189-205.

93. Padilla and Phan, *Theology of Migration*, 1.

94. Pagán 2013:44.

95. Pope Benedict XVI, *Questions and Answers* (Huntington: Our Sunday Visitor, 2008), 21.

96. Manchala 2014:157.

In Zambia, during the events of xenophobia in April 2016,[97] the mainline churches and the Catholic Church worked effectively together in addressing this issue. In working and coordinating together, the churches became places of refuge and hosting of refugees and migrants.[98] This experience was not particular to Zambia alone; in 2008, the Central Methodist Mission in central Johannesburg, South Africa, took in refugees after the spread of xenophobic violence in South Africa. The churches not only provided shelter to the victims, but also they provided material support based on the church's quest to respect human life and promote social justice.[99]

In addition, the Pietermaritzburg Cluster of Theological Institutions, an ecumenical body in South Africa which provides many opportunities for ecumenical exchange, is still accomplishing another ecumenical endeavour. The cluster, through liturgical celebrations, conferences, and publications, stands always against xenophobia as part of walking together toward the existential peripheries. Although much effort has been made ecumenically, there is still an urgent need to address the issue of migration together as Christians. The effort of addressing migration together is what Pope John Paul II called "an exchange of gifts"[100] because it is an exchange, it cannot be carried out alone.

Conclusion

This essay has shown an integral relationship among material poverty, a political war situation, and migration. The migrants' journey of humility and humiliation (kenosis) is not a problem but an opportunity for the churches to "rediscover themselves afresh"[101] and to witness together. As a way of concluding, we embrace the three levels of acting toward migration as proposed by Groody: "pastoral level, the spiritual level, and theological level."[102] The pastoral level consists in offering assistance on the pilgrim journey. It requires the churches to advocate for legislative advocacy which

---

97. *Zambia Weekly 2016* reports that Saint Ignatius Catholic Church in Lusaka received more than 300 people from Rwanda, Burundi, and the Democratic Republic of the Congo who sought protection.

98. N. Mwale, J. Chita, J 2016. The Church's Social Responsibility in Zambia: The Catholic Response to the 2017 Prejudiced Attacks on 'Others'. (University of Zambia: Lusaka. Alternation Special Edition 19, 2017) 132 – 156.Mwale and Chita, *The Church's Social Responsibility in Zambia*, 134–35.

99. Ibid., 146.

100. Pope John Paul II, *Ut Unum Sint* (Nairobi: Pauline, 1995), 28.

101. Manchala 2014:164.

102. Groody 2013:140.

fight a xenophobic mentality and provide material support toward migrants. Becoming friends on the journey and sharing meals should be the focus. The spiritual level, in Groody's mind, "has less to do with giving and more to do with listening."[103] It requires a quality of presence toward the migrants, listening to their inner lives and their deep thoughts, empowering them to overcome challenges encountered. The theological level indicates that migration is a journey, "a fundamental movement from God and return to God."[104] On this journey, migrants are at risk of losing everything, including their lives and their faith.[105] As people on pilgrimage, the church is called to walk and work with and for migrants, bringing healing grace in spreading the good news. This last aspect looks at migration eschatologically with the lenses of hope. Migration is not only going forth but also homecoming[106] and passing from death into everlasting life.

------

103. Ibid., 140.
104. Ibid., 141.
105. Groody 2013:149.
106. Irvin 2014:18.

Political Hindrance to Justice, Peace and Economic Growth in Zimbabwe: With Special Reference to Its Failed Execution of Land Reform Programmes and Mining-Induced Displacement, 2000–2011

Mberikwazvo Ian Chitambo

Abstract

Politics marked with honesty and truth is vital for justice, peace, and economic growth. There is a need for introspection: rectifying past hurts, unveiling present obstacles, and looking at avenues for a future that will achieve prosperous societies marked with uprightness. This essay, using an approach of analysis, synthesis, and engagement, will analyze the Fast Track Land Reform Programme of 2000 and the Chiadzwa Mining-Induced Displacement of 2011 in Zimbabwe. The former presaged economic crisis and massive humanitarian injustices, and the latter was replete with injustices shielded by an unpitying political regime. The author will engage with these events and offer recommendations.

Introduction

There are great opportunities for growth in Zimbabwe. However, certain issues must be looked at objectively before embarking on the project of growth. When one surveys and sees the state of Zimbabwe, one will echo Wingo's words that "there is no denial that our new African nation-states today, as yesteryear, face deep political and consequently economic and social pathologies such as a lack of trust, of democratic freedom, of rule of law, and of the accountability of the government to the governed."[1] First, this essay seeks to unveil the social pathologies in Zimbabwe which lie in a failed political system. The first part seeks to separate the real issues – lack of peace and justice – from the not-so-real issues that take centre stage in Zimbabwean politics: marketing a peaceful Zimbabwe that is open for investment. Second, the essay will map out the real issues using the Zimbabwean historical context of the land reform programmes and the

---

1. A.H. Wingo, "Fellowship Associations as a Foundation for Liberal Democracy in Africa," in K. Wiredu, ed., *A Companion to African Philosophy* (Malden: Blackwell, 2004), 450.

mining-induced displacement in Chiadzwa. It will then look at the socio-economic effects of these programmes. Third, the essay will look at how the Catholic Church has responded to such social issues, particularly the Catholic Church in Zimbabwe from 2000 to 2011. Lastly, the essay will offer some concrete steps that could be taken for justice and peace to prevail.

The Not-So-Real Issues

Pope Francis, challenging consecrated men and women during the Year of Consecrated Life (2015), said, "realities are more important than ideas ... Realities simply are, whereas ideas are worked out. There has to be a continuous dialogue between the two, lest ideas become detached from realities. It is dangerous to dwell in the realm of words alone, of images and rhetoric."[2] In the same line, going about social issues in Zimbabwe can be clouded by various facets and rhetorical methodology that, in many instances, take centre stage at the expense of the real issues. For instance, the mission could be reduced to efforts and determination to present a positive Zimbabwe to the whole world. Although this effort is warranted, it should not drift from the core issues that are the cause of the much-lamented continual disintegration of Zimbabwean communities. This is also apparent in most African countries: there is a reaction against a negatively publicized Africa which has resulted in an approach of marketing a positive Africa. This could also be true of the Christian churches in Africa. Church leaders in Africa pray for peace, seek dialogue, and speak of a beautiful Africa which has potential for growth. All of these are great efforts, but if they do not hinge on the real issues in Africa, there is no hope; there will be no growth, and religion could be justly termed the opium of the masses in African societies such as Zimbabwe.

Facing the Real Issues

What is important is not what people think about Zimbabwe but what Zimbabwe communicates to the world. What is communicated is not found in expensive conferences that Zimbabwean leaders host to attract investors. The behaviour, poverty, migration rates, political instabilities, conflicts, and corruption evident in Zimbabwe are enough communication to the world. Poverty reveals that humanitarian rights principles have been dishonoured by the political order of the day. The real issues in Zimbabwe are evident in the

---

2. Congregation for Institutes of Consecrated Life and Societies of Apostolic Life, *New Wine in New Wineskins* (Nairobi: Paulines Publications Africa, 2018), 6.

lack of peace and justice.[3] As Bennet says, "Peace is not just the absence of violence. Where societies are affected by a culture of suspicion and fear, there is no true peace. Where there are glaring inequalities and people's dignity and rights are being abused, there is false peace." The humanitarian terms "law," "justice," and "rights" should be at the core of the discussion in the Zimbabwean context. In many instances, political leaders and some church leaders have failed the masses; there is an explicit fear of opening up the crypt that houses skeletons of humanitarian problems in Zimbabwe. The Africa we pray for, Zimbabwe in particular, must connect with where we are coming from, where we are, and where we hope to be. First of all, there is need to address the real issue of a political system that has disintegrated and a social order that is rapidly becoming disoriented. Our fundamental problem is how to find ways of establishing wellbeing for all: this has been neglected through celebrating pseudo successes in Zimbabwe that are in many instances marked with loss of blood and also marked by a church losing its prophetic voice.

Mapping the Real Issues of Justice and Peace within the Historical Context of Zimbabwe and Its Land Programmes

The Land Reform Programme 2000

Zimbabwe has the most contested land reform programme (LRP) on the continent. To some, it was a well-executed programme, and to some it was a failed exercise. Gonese et al. remark that "historical inequalities in Zimbabwe demanded action by the government and its citizens … 42% of the land in Zimbabwe (being marginally productive and drought prone land) was reserved for blacks, while 51% (being the more fertile, better watered, more productive and better serviced regions of the country) was technically if not explicitly reserved for whites."[4] It was evident that the proportions were not fair. After independence, the Zimbabwean government saw it as just and fit to redistribute the land. The government then set up land redistribution programmes that were guided by laws. However, these models did not last long.

---

3. M. Bennett, *Faith and Social Justice* (Nairobi: Paulines Publications Africa, 2012), 75.

4. Francis T. Gonese, Nelson Marongwe, Charles M. Mukora and Bill Kinsey, *Land Reform and Resettlement Implementation in Zimbabwe: An Overview of the Programme against Selected International Experiences* (2002), 8, https://minds.wisconsin.edu/bitstream/handle/1793/23060/ LRRPOverview.pdf. Gonese et al. do not account for the other 7 percent.

The year 2000 saw the beginning of a Fast Track Land Reform Programme (FTLRP). Cliffe explains that the "Land Acquisition Act 2000, plus regulations proclaimed after enabling changes in the constitution, allowed for compulsory acquisition without compensation for the value of the land itself."[5] The FTLRP was marked by gruesome government-tolerated violence that saw beatings, killings, rape, and the displacement of many white farmers and their workers. From 2001 on, Zimbabwe quickly entered into an economic crisis. During this period, there was no clear separation of the ruling party, the legislature, the government (as a civil entity), and the judiciary.

Mining-induced Displacement in Chiadzwa, Zimbabwe, in 2011

Another land programme that would see the displacement of people came with the discovery of diamonds in Chiadzwa, in the Manicaland province. Madebwe et al. note that diamonds had been discovered in this area as early as 2002, but there were disagreements about who was to mine them.[6] Unofficial mining by locals started in 2006.[7] Mbada Diamonds, the company that was contracted to mine, came in and began an official mining programme in late 2010. It proposed a resettlement programme that would see over 600 households being moved to make way for mining processes. This was meant to be a developmental-induced displacement. The families to be displaced were to be relocated and compensated for their land, unmovable assets, loss of income, and so forth. The resettlement happened and each family was allocated 10 hectares of dry farmland far from their ancestral lands, $1,000 USD, and the promise of groceries worth between $400 and $480 USD per month for at least four months. In addition, each family was allocated 1 hectare of irrigable land. This was not enough; Madebwe et al. say that according to the valuation of the displaced families, the people estimated that they lost between $25,000 and $30,000 USD, which they asked to be compensated for.[8] The company was to engage with the resettled people, but this never occurred. The government was in partnership with the diamond

---

5. Lionel Cliffe, Jocelyn Alexander, Ben Cousins and Rudo Gaidsanwa, "An Overview of Fast Track Land Reform in Zimbabwe: Editorial Introduction," *Journal of Peasant Studies* 38: 5 (2011), 907–38, at 912.

6. Crescentia Madebwe, Victor Madebwe and Sophia Mavusa, "Involuntary Displacement and Resettlement to Make Way for Diamond Mining: The Case of Chiadzwa Villagers in Marange, Zimbabwe," *Journal of Research in Peace, Gender and Development* 1: 10 (2011), 292–301, at 293.

7. The locals believed it was a gift from their ancestors and that they had a right to gain from these diamonds.

8. Madebwe et al., "Involuntary Displacement and Resettlement," 296.

mining company, and it was evident that the government did not take the compensation issue seriously. Many abuses by the army were recorded, mainly by independent media outlets; to date, the relocated families have not been duly compensated. Mwonzora argues that the Zimbabwean government titled these displacements development induced, while human rights organizations argue that on the contrary, it was abuse.[9]

Socio-economic Issues: Effects of these Land Programmes

Mwonzora notes that "most displacements that have taken place in Zimbabwe have not been predictable, open and fair and have not resulted in the just treatment of the evicted or displaced people."[10] The economic programmes should serve the people, rather than the people serving the economic programmes. The consequences of these programmes still haunt many Zimbabweans, and for many they have been the cause of the deplorable situations that most Zimbabweans within and outside Zimbabwe are experiencing. The FTLRP has been identified, on top of the economic sanctions on Zimbabwe, as the cause of the dire economic situation that the country is in. Land which was productive was, in many cases, taken by people who had no farming or business management skills and who went on to plunder resources. The government further instructed the Reserve Bank of Zimbabwe to dish out huge amounts to war veterans who had acquired land from the FTLRP; the money was not used for agricultural purposes. This further increased the crisis in Zimbabwe. Gumede notes that "the effect of Zimbabwe's failed land reform programme is clear. According to the United Nations children's agency around 3 million Zimbabweans need regularly food aid. Around 40% of Zimbabwean households are hungry."[11]

Such conditions make people feel unsafe in Zimbabwe. For most, migrating presented hope for a better livelihood. Every person has a right to migrate, but the right to stay in one's country is more cherished and desired. Yet choosing to stay reveals signs of violated rights in all spheres. Zimbabwe has one of the highest rates of migration in Africa, mostly to its neighbour South Africa. There remains no hope in Zimbabwe due to the failed economy.

---

9. D. Mwonzora, "'Diamond Rush' and the Relocation of the Chiadzwa Community in Zimbabwe: A Human Rights Perspective," MA thesis, Graduate School of Development Studies, The Hague, 2011, 15.

10. Ibid., 2.

11. William Gumede, "Lessons from Zimbabwe's Failed Land Reforms," News 24, 14 October 2018, https://www.news24.com/news24/columnists/guestcolumn/lessons-from-zimbabwes-failed-land-reforms-20181014.

The mass migration in Zimbabwe is mainly economic and political. The FTLRP and the Chiadzwa displacement significantly added to the Zimbabwean mass migration. Crush and Tevera report that mass out-migration would seem to be a perfectly predictable consequence of Zimbabwe's economic and social collapse.[12] In 2000, the year of the FTLRP, around 500,000 people crossed legally from Zimbabwe into South Africa, including about 64,261 white Zimbabweans. For the Chiadzwa people, no migration numbers have been recorded, but those who remained where they had been resettled were few; the young generation especially went to find greener pastures elsewhere.

What was evident here was the lack of economic justice, which calls for fairness in the distribution of resources. The government replicated the colonial system they sought to fight; they did not execute these programmes to benefit all. The beneficiaries of the land programmes mentioned above were an elite minority, affiliated to the ruling party, which gained at the expense of the greater majority that were meant to gain from the programmes: the poor did not benefit from these, and among the exploited were women. Cliffe et al., in relation to the FTLRP, say there were

> narrow openings for women to be granted land officially in their own right … women farmers who managed to get use of land have often had to acquire it indirectly and by wheedling it out of spouses or wider family or political influentials; and having got land have difficulty in utilising it fully, experiencing the usual problems of scarcity of inputs, draught power, water, labour and secure tenure even more severely than men.[13]

In the broader society, Okin identifies women and children as those who have lived terrifyingly close to economic disaster and serious social displacement; many also suffer violence and the recurring threat of it.[14] The land programmes in Zimbabwe, modelled by patriarchal power, which knows no limits in squandering, subjugated women. There was no economic justice among both sexes. In the FTLRP, as seen above, the redistribution neglected women; the Chiadzwa displacements saw female-headed families at a great disadvantage of claiming land rights, and thus in turn compensation.

---

12. Jonathan Crush and Daniel Tevera, eds, *Zimbabwe's Exodus: Crisis, Migration, Survival* (Cape Town: Southern African Migration Programme, 2010), 8.

13. Cliffe et al., *An Overview of Fast Track Land Reform in Zimbabwe*, 919.

14. S. Moller Okin, "The Family: Gender and Justice," in *Social Justice*, ed. M. Clayton and A. Williams (Malden: Blackwell, 1989), 211.

Catholic Social Teaching

When it comes to issues pertaining to humanitarian rights, the Catholic Church links the issues to its social teaching. With its deep roots tracing back to the early Christian communities, the Catholic Church has always been concerned with social issues and shows how humanity should honour values and principles that respect humanitarian rights. The church seeks to help people resist and fight injustices; this is done through the writings of the popes, councils, and national bishops' conferences. In this light, the Zimbabwean Catholic Bishops' Conference (ZCBC) has tried to address social issues in the country. In 1997, the conference issued a pastoral letter, *ZCBC Statement on Land Reform*, which predates the FTLRP. The aim was to initiate a discourse with the government. The ZCBC had cautioned the government in the land reform programme it was seeking to undertake, noting some basic requirements that would result in equality, fairness, and justice:[15]

> Catholic social teaching has never portrayed private property rights as absolute. If it is for the common good, expropriation of land is allowed.[16] However, expropriation of land or displacements that involve land should be executed within a framework that ensures that those whose land is taken are compensated justly.

At the core of Catholic social teaching and all the documents mentioned above is the preferential option for the poor, which seeks to give love and a voice to the poor. It encourages the building of a healthy society where the poor are given priority: the necessary resources, skills, and knowledge that will enable them to be self-reliant. In 2011, the year of the Chiadzwa mining-induced displacement, the ZCBC did not produce a document specifically addressing this issue. However, it did publish *Let Us Work for the Common Good*, which addressed the government's neglect of the poor, including those who were displaced in Chiadzwa. The bishops urged the government to "prioritize poverty eradication by using proceeds from natural resources like diamonds,

---

15. Zimbabwe Catholic Bishops' Conference, *Statement on Land Reform* (Harare: ZCBC Publications, 1997), 112.

16. Pope Paul VI, in Populorum Progressio (The Development of Peoples), states that "the right to private property is not absolute" and "if certain land estates impede the general prosperity … the common good sometimes demands their expropriation." Human rights should be respected, and those whose land is expropriated should be allowed to continue with a good life. Pope Paul VI, *Populorum Progressio* (Rome: Libreria Editrice Vaticana, 1967), 23–24.

land, etc., for the development of the whole nation and all its citizens."[17]

Despite this erudite Catholic social teaching, some could argue that the Catholic Church, in certain cases, has been informative instead of performative in its call for equality between the sexes, challenging civil authorities and encouraging renewal. The Catholic Church itself, in practice, is very slow to implement some of its ideas. One example is discrimination against women. In *Pacem in Terris* (Peace on Earth) Pope John XXIII said,

> every human being has a natural right to be respected, a right to a good
> name, a right to freedom in investigating the truth, and within the limits
> of the moral order and the common good to freedom of speech and publi-
> cation, and to freedom to pursue whatever profession they may choose. He
> has the right, also, to be accurately informed about public events.[18]

The church has been slow in allowing women, who are the majority of the church, to be in decision-making positions, despite their willingness to contribute to matters that affect them. Some have also argued that the church underuses its lands and is reluctant to sell or surrender them to the civil authorities for the common good.

Concrete Steps toward Transforming Injustices and Violence

Reconciliation: An Avenue to Renewal

The FTLRP and Chiadzwa displacements in Zimbabwe call for a process of reconciliation. Dombo states that "the truth and reconciliation process can free a society from its obsession with past injustices, redirecting political debate to contemporary issues."[19] With a reconciled spirit, people can engage in dialogue toward renewal. However, this should not just be rhetoric, which has been the mark of Zimbabwean talks on reconciliation. There should be evident signs of moving toward true reconciliation marked by compensation for lost land or improvements that were done on expropriated land, compensation for victims of state-induced violence, the acknowledging of past mistakes by perpetrators, and a willing heart to forgive past hurts. Bennet acknowledges that "future generations of Zimbabweans will also have

17. Zimbabwe Catholic Bishops' Conference, *Let Us Work for the Common Good* (Harare: ZCBC Publications, 2011), 343.

18. Pope John XXIII, *Pacem in Terris* (Washington: USCCB, 1963), 12.

19. S. Dombo, "Refusing to be Co-opted? Church Organizations and Reconciliation in Zimbabwe, with Special Reference to the Christian Alliance of Zimbabwe 2005–2013," *Journal for the Study of Religion* 27: 2 (2014), 137–71, at 139.

to deal with traumatic events since land occupation began in 2000. It is easily forgotten that most of the 320 000 farm workers (and their families) who were

in the farms before the occupations began lost their jobs and their homes in the displacement."[20] There is need for a true process that looks at the past, amid errors and failures, and in turn seeks forgiveness. This will mark a nation embarking on a healing process of renewal. In this process, a theory of justice as fairness as proposed by Rawls[21] can best serve the procedure. Those who set up such a theory should not be knowing the sex, class position, or social status of the recipients. This will enable a fair distribution of goods that does not exclude groups like the poor, women, and children, as has been the case in Zimbabwe in the past.

Reconciliation should not only be demanded among persons, but also for the environment, which has been abused, neglected, and exploited. In *Laudato Si'* (Praise Be to You), on the environment, Pope Francis says, "this sister now cries out to us because of the harm we have inflicted on her by our irresponsible use and abuse of the goods with which God has endowed her. We have come to see ourselves as her lords and masters, entitled to plunder her at will."[22] The violence present in the Zimbabwean society, wounded by sin, is also reflected in the indications of catastrophes evident in the soil, in the water, in the air, and in all forms of life. Greediness in Zimbabwe led to the destruction of the environment: for example, trees were cut down to make way for mining, with no official plan to plant more trees. There is an urgent need for people – especially the government, which has neglected both people and the environment, to push for a reconciliation program that will enable the protection of natural resources and appropriate use of them.

Breaking the Practice of Silence: The Prophetic Call of the Church

Kinunda poses questions to contemporary ministers in the face of the urgent need for justice and peace, saying, "are we able, in this environment of the 'African Renaissance', to be prophetic catalysts in forging a new image for a new continent that is emerging from centuries of both external as a well as internal degradation and abuse? Who is going to be the 'Jeremiah' of

---

20. Bennett, *Faith and Social Justice*, 77.

21. John Rawls, "Justice as Fairness" (1985), 3, http://fs2.american.edu/dfagel/www/ Philosophers/Rawls/JusticeAsFairnessAbridged.pdf.

22. Pope Francis, Laudato Si' (Nairobi: Paulines Publication Africa, 2015), 2.

the 'African Renaissance' if not the pastoral agent and minister today?"[23] The most important heritage of prophets for our modern context is a call for social justice: faith involves the pursuit of fairness and justice in the civic domain that is political, economic, and judicial. Bennett gives an outline and examples of what the Old Testament prophets were meant to do: "prophets protest against the outrages committed against the poor by the rich and powerful (cf. Is 3:15; Am 4:32-37; 5:12; Ez 22:29). They stridently condemn those who use political power, economic and religious authority for their own selfish ends (Is 59:6-8)."[24] Jesus continued with the same prophetic outcry in his time, exposing, through his ministry, the tyrannical political systems that oppressed God's people and leaders who created an economic environment that disadvantaged many for their own gain. These areas are often pigeonholed today as being irreligious and not the concern of people of faith.[25]

If the church is to have that prophetic voice, as a body of Christ, it should be united[26] without fear to expose these ills, to inform the consciences of its members who have power to remedy political ills. Bennet argues that "the prophets understand that the earth and its resources were created by God for all to share and must not be appropriated by individuals or groups in an exclusive way. Human beings are stewards of creation rather than its owners."[27] Conversely, the church's task of challenging social injustices

---

23. Q. Kinunda, "Resource for Pauline Literature and Prophets," unpublished lecture notes (Cedara: SJTI, 2016), 84.

24. Bennett, *Faith and Social Justice,* 43.

25. In 2016, President Robert Mugabe threatened a pastor, Evan Mawarire, against meddling in what he termed "political matters" after Mawarire called for justice and a stop to political brutality in Zimbabwean society. In the early 2000s, Mugabe threatened a Catholic archbishop, Pius Ncube.

26. Zimbabwe has had many examples of disunity that led the church not to have a prophetic voice against a government that does not respect life and the common good for all. Dombo reports on how the church failed in its role during the 2008 elections, which were marked with abuses and irregular voting systems: he says, "the church didn't have a united voice as some churches had been apparently co-opted by Mugabe, especially Reverend Obadiah Musindo of the Destiny for Africa Network, Nolbert Kunonga of the Anglican Church and members of the African Initiated Churches of Johannes Marange and Masowe. This problem of churches being co-opted by politicians was also noted by the ZCBC, the EFZ and the ZCC in their national vision document, where they noted that some Church members had fallen into the pit of political appeasement at the expense of maintaining the integrity of the Church. They noted that divisions within the Church based on differences of political affiliation and/or sympathies were hindering the Church from providing a more coherent and unified voice of leadership to the nation." Dombo, "Refusing to be Co-opted?" 153.

27. Bennett, *Faith and Social Justice,* 43.

should be carried out by both men and women and avoid the reciprocity that has been there between man and woman in the mission of the church. The Vatican's Congregation for Institutes of Consecrated Life and Societies of Apostolic Life argues that "multiple one-sided prejudices in both society and the Church have prevented the recognition of the gifts of the true feminine genius"[28] women, who in most instances are the ones affected by poverty and violence, should have a voice in fighting against injustices, and platforms within the church should be opened for them to speak on behalf of the church.

Looking at the cycle of oppression, going from one form of tyranny to another, one can easily be left in despair at the migration figures in Zimbabwe: people are slowly giving up hope. However, there should be hope that things will change. This hope is fostered in the belief that God does not abandon his people and that God's word, which does not change, calls for social justice. The church, in challenging social injustices, should not leave people in despair; it should give them a renewed hope.

Adopting Governance Systems that Allow Justice and Peace to Reign

Nyong'o says, "there is a definite correlation between the lack of democratic practices in African politics and the deteriorating economic condition … questions of development and problems of economic crises" – and to this can be added justice, peace, and, in the face of the current COVID-19 pandemic, good health-care systems – "cannot therefore be meaningfully discussed without discussing problems regarding the nature of state."[29] At the core of all improvement, renewal, and change lies the willingness of political players to be on board. This calls for a review of how politics has served the interests of the masses in Zimbabwe. Zimbabwe has experienced a failed governance system: party politics. Just before the toppling of Robert Mugabe in 2017, the masses had wished for his downfall. Mere months after his "resignation," the attention and blame shifted to the current president, Mnangagwa. The problem, as this essay argues, does not lie with sitting presidents: it is the problem of an inherited system of governance (party politics) that does not suit the needs and metaphysical makeup of the people it seeks to serve.

---

28. Congregation for Institutes of Consecrated Life and Societies of Apostolic Life, *New Wine in New Wineskins*, 17.

29. Peter A. Nyong'o, "Popular Struggles for Democracy in Africa," in B. Caron et al., eds, *Democratic Transition in Africa* (Ibadan: Credu, 1992), 360.

With party politics, there has been evidence of military and police services intimidating, beating, and killing for political ends. This has been the experience of those who have challenged the Zimbabwean government by calling for justice on the FTLRP. Also, the judiciary has ignored compensation claims by displaced people in Chiadzwa. In most cases, perpetrators of these violent acts are not prosecuted or sentenced. Party politics does not show the democracy that is purported by its devotees. The word "democracy" comes from two Greek words: *demos*, meaning "full citizens living within a particular city-state," and *kratos*, meaning "power" or "rule." This was expressed plainly in Abraham Lincoln's definition of democracy: "government of the people, by the people, for the people." The nature of party politics is that most, if not all, leaders serve the needs of their parties and to some extent of their tribal kinsmen before the needs of society at large.

Wiredu suggested a political system that seeks consensus among political parties.[30] This system, as Ani states, will allow a more inclusive approach compared to mere voting.[31] This might appear to be nostalgia at work, wishing to bring back the traditional system of governance into our modern era – an idea that might be met with a fair amount of resistance. However, we cannot ignore the fact that the modern practice of party politics and majoritarian democracy has failed in Zimbabwe. The numbers game cannot fix the issues the country faces. Lauer gives examples of people who have called Wiredu's idea romantic, illusory, and a fantasy: reaching consensus over majoritarian democracy cannot be easily achieved, if it can be achieved at all.[32] Wiredu conceded that consensus does not entail total agreement; diversity is evident in it, but dialogue can smooth the edges. People involved in deliberations can make decisions out of agreement without necessarily having to lose their opinions on what ought to be done. Wiredu therefore sees consensus as the quest for the common good, which recognizes that all human interests are ultimately the same. As he says, "consensus is not just an optional bonus …

---

30. K. Wiredu, "Democracy and Consensus in African Traditional Politics: A Plea for Non-party Polity," in Postcolonial African Philosophy: *A Critical Reader*, ed E.C. Eze (Oxford: Blackwell, 1997), 310.

31. E.I. Ani, "On Traditional African Consensual Rationality," The Journal of Political Philosophy 33: 3 (2013), 311–20, at 311. The inclusive government of Zimbabwe, Government of National Unity, can work as an example, where people began to dialogue for the betterment of the nation.

32. H. Lauer, "Negotiating Pre-colonial History and Future Democracy: Kwasi Wiredu and his critics," in Identity Meets Nationality: Voices from the Humanities, eds. H. Lauer et al (Legon: Sub-Saharan Publishers, 2011) 177.

it is essential for securing substantive, or what might be called decisional, representation for representatives and, through them, for the citizens at large. This is nothing short of a matter of fundamental human rights."[33] Consensus therefore calls for a political system led by inclusiveness of all parties in decision making: government.

Thabo Mbeki, during the conference on Partnership Africa in Sweden in 1997, noted that Africans have achieved political emancipation from colonial and white minority domination.[34] Despite this great achievement, they have failed to eradicate the most grievous problems that faced the people in the time of colonialism. With whatever systems they have experimented on, as a form of governance, all that has been achieved is "the establishment of one-party states, the resort to military rule, the dependence for our development on the charity of others wealthier than ourselves, counting on their altruism." In a nutshell, one can safely say that democracy is not defended or evident in party politics as manifested in Zimbabwe, and that consensus could be the hope for Zimbabwean politics.[35]

Conclusion

The struggle continues. "As Africans we have a vision, a hope, a prayer about what will come in the end."[36] Whatever comes in the end in Zimbabwe should be the new Zimbabwe, open for business in the full sense that is evidenced by justice, equality, freedom, and respect for human rights. Zimbabwe has great potential, and many Zimbabweans are working for a better Zimbabwe. However, all these efforts are marred by corruption, abuse of political power, and a political system that does not serve the interests of all. Policies can be set up, but they cannot succeed in an unfavourable environment. As seen in the example of Zimbabwe, which had set up good land reform programmes and mining-induced displacements, if these were carried out with an effective implementation marked by rule of law and social justice, it would have been a success story; however, greed, corruption, and a failed political system hindered such developments.

---

33. Wiredu, "Democracy and Consensus," 310.

34. T. Mbeki, *Africa: The Time Has Come* (Cape Town: Tafelberg, 1998), 206.

35. The Zimbabwe Heads of Christian Denominations met on 7 October 2019 to call for a Sabbath: to put a halt on all political contestation for a period of seven years for the ruling party and the main opposition party to find a collaborative working system to address the economic crisis in Zimbabwe. This is a sign of how non-party politics is important for Zimbabwe.

36. Mbeki, *Africa*, 201.

This essay has challenged the church to be an agent of change, having the courage to speak out, united in one voice, building up Christ's kingdom, and giving tomorrow's generation reason and hope to live in Zimbabwe and for Zimbabwe. This will lead to a reduction in migration rates, respect for the environment, gender equality, and political practice aimed at the common good. Rev. Mwombeki, during his acceptance speech after his induction as general secretary at the 11th General Assembly of the All Africa Conference of Churches, said, "My Africa is a continent of hope, a continent on the rise."[37] Applied to Zimbabwe, this statement shows that Zimbabwe is not doomed to be eternally a sad story; there are ills that are evident and should be challenged and fixed so it can turn over a new leaf and explode in its growth. This is the Zimbabwe I pray for.

37. F. Mwombeki, "Rev. Dr. Fidon Mwombeki Acceptance Speech after Induction," All Africa Conference of Churches, 7 July 2018, http://www.aacc-ceta.org/en/news/25-rev-dr-fidon-mwombeki-acceptance-speech-after-induction.

5

Justice for the "Hustler Generation": A Case Study of the Green Anglican Movement in the Kenya Anglican Youth Organization

Godfrey Owino Adera

Abstract

This essay explores a mission praxis for the church in dealing with rapid unemployment for youth in Kenya. Youth on the quest for a decent livelihood are popularly described as "hustlers" in Kenya. A case study of the Green Anglican movement in the Kenya Anglican Youth Organization is explored. Employing a missional praxis model, the essay argues that the church can be an affirming space for hustlers by creating more hustles (especially on mitigating ecological crises) for youth and advocating for licensing, affirmation, integration, and harnessing of various youth hustles into the formal sector of the economy. It suggests mainstreaming the youth agenda in a programmatic model for the church in Kenya as an appropriate response in the church's pilgrimage and quest for justice with youth in the context of rapid unemployment.

Introduction

The word "hustler" has become common in Kenya, but its context is vague. The word itself has a negative connotation from dictionary meanings related to someone who jostles, pushes, acts roughly, bumps, knocks, sells aggressively, and works as a prostitute. Politicians have used the word to refer to leaders who have come from poor backgrounds and, through resilience and fortitude, have become successful and well placed.[1] On the other hand, they have used the same term to refer to politicians whom they perceive as swindlers who siphon public coffers for selfish gains and give out handouts to pacify the public and to church fundraisers to sanitize their greed.[2] However, many unemployed graduates and youth in general prefer this term

---

1. Too Godfrey, "Ruto Hits at Raila for Calling Him Hustler," March 2019 https://www.pulselive.co.ke/news/politics/dp-ruto-rants-with-hard-hitting-remarks-targetting-raila-after-the-odm-boss-mocked/xb6qygx.

2. Ann Mkenya, "Raila Mocks Hustler, DP Ruto on a Ranting Spree," 2 March 2019, https://youtu.be/NfoIVnVf0UU.

in qualifying their informal and very necessary ventures of making ends meet. It simply defines the engagement in diverse income-earning activities among educated Kenyan youth who are increasingly faced with uncertainties in formal employment.

One can, however, deduce that this is not a word against which a progressive society ought to benchmark its value system to guarantee a dependable future generation, as based on the term "hustler generation." For instance, Ben Omollo observes that in Kenya, over and above the negative synonyms, the word is underpinned with impunity and a "me first" self-entitlement mentality, which is interwoven with the thread of the end justifying the means.[3] He further notes that the evident signal of the hustler mentality is the fast depletion of a stock of role models whom the youth can look up to, since a person can go from being honoured as an accomplished professional and leader and then be exposed as being part of sour public deals and a self-interested narrative.[4] According to Omollo, corruption, competition, and greed, all imbued in selfish interests, are the harbingers of this connotation. Omollo's arguments are representative of many critiques which have been raised by several opinion leaders in the private, public, and even religious sectors in Kenya.[5]

The fact that "hustler" – as a word and a social location – has become an obvious yet vague response among many Kenyans when asked what they do for a living demands an inquiry. The study pays attention to the use of the term by the youth themselves to assert a positive self-concept and aspirations. Thus, "the hustler generation" is an appropriate taxonomy in this discourse. Hustling here implies a nexus of the adaptability and flexibility of youth inspired by neoliberal reforms and the resulting socioeconomic uncertainties. Generally, many young Kenyans may mean well when they respond that they are hustlers. The contextual vagueness of the response best explains their informal and very necessary ventures or hustles of making ends meet. They are simply a crop of hard-working, innovative, creative, and resilient people with a visible desire and intent to progress in life, yet are sandwiched within the tag of extortionists, swindlers, busybodies, and lazy people in a context where the purpose for living becomes critical after graduating. Thus, I consider the hustler generation as an appropriate taxonomy in both a broad and an objective sense.

---

3. Ben Omollo, 2017, "Kenya Is a Country of Hustlers and It Hurts," *Public Finance Governance Magazine* (May 2017), 9–12.

4. Ibid.

5. "The Sonkonization of Kenya, Best PLO Lumumba Speech Ever," 6 August 2018, https://youtu.be/_4tT8TUz724.

As used broadly, the term encompasses all the activities that unemployed graduates engage in as part of their quest for a dignified life. In this manner, they are victims, people trapped in a cage where they must manage and fulfil societal expectations and personal ambitions in education and earning a living. Sadly, the outcome-based curriculum, of which they are products, glorifies graduation as a ticket for employment and subsequently for prosperity, wellness, and wealth. They are subjects, human capital who spin the wheel of innovation, create self-employment and jobs, and foster local economies. They increasingly invent new subjectivities that enable them to manoeuvre the changing labour markets and creatively reconstruct their aspirations through a range of activities. Grace Muthoni Mwaura describes this as "side-hustling."[6] As such, youth engage in diverse income-earning activities because they are increasingly faced with formal employment uncertainties.[7] Hustling offers the hustler generation an alternative livelihood strategy, a means for self-improvement, and a reconfiguration of their imagined futures.

This study provides a concretization of this perspective within a church context in relation to both economic justice and ecological concerns. The first section provides background to situate the hustling concept within the youth populace: specifically, graduates. Generally, the quest for justice among this populace is carried through memes. The second section analyzes missional praxis as the framework for this study. The third section shows the Anglican Church of Kenya's response to rapid unemployment. This response is two-fold and involves the creation of hustles for youth through environmental stewardship and advocacy for ecofriendly technologies and activities. The former addresses the economic viability and potency of the youth's creativity and innovativeness in mitigating the effects of environmental degradation. The latter addresses policies and the involvement of youth as key stakeholders in caring for the earth. In so doing, programmatic responses to ecological injustice become a church-initiated hustle (economic justice) for the hustler generation.

---

6. Grace Muthoni Mwaura, "The Side-Hustle: Diversified Livelihoods of Kenyan Educated Young Farmers," I*DS Bulletin* 48: 3 (2017), 18–46.

7. Ibid.

Background to the Study

One issue that has sparked a lot of debate in Kenya in the recent past is the Citizen TV exposé called "First-class Betrayal."[8] In this exposé, a university graduate named Kevin Ochieng, who went to the best schools in Kenya, topped the country in high school, and graduated with first-class honours in actuarial science becomes a street person because he could not get a job. This story is just the tip of the iceberg: thousands of bright unemployed graduates struggle to make ends meet. This is evident from the plethora of reactions that this story sparked both in public discussions and on social media. For instance, the hashtag *#FirstclassBetrayal* started trending within an hour, with many young people sharing their similar experiences, posting their resumés for whoever might want to see them, and expressing their frustrations with a dysfunctional economic regime.[9]

Generally, unemployment in Kenya has become a menace for those in leadership and those seeking jobs. Every year, thousands of young Kenyans graduate from universities and start jostling for employment opportunities. Although successive governments have tried to mitigate this alarming situation, the labour supply has been on the rise in relation to demand. This has created a huge backlog; the impact is felt by the youth who seek to get returns for their investment in education. Based on this fact, this paper defines unemployment in terms of the supply-and-demand phenomenon. It considers Keynes, Pribram and Phelan's (1946) and Madan's (1965) definitions of unemployment as applicable. Pribam states that unemployment occurs when the supply of labour power exceeds the demand for that labour force.[10] Madan similarly notes that unemployment is the dearth of opportunities of jobs for people willing to work and actively looking for a job.[11]

Whereas the International Labour Organization (ILO) defines youth as people aged 15 to 24,[12] which is corroborated by the United Nations,[13] this

---

8. Kenya Citizen TV, "First Class Betrayal: First class graduate lives on the streets," 21 July 2019, https://youtu.be/PA0aotr9MVo.

9. Ibid.

10. John Maynard Keynes, Karl Pribram and E.J. Phelan, *Unemployment as a World-Problem* (Chicago: University of Chicago Press, 1946).

11. Lal Pur Madan, *On the Estimation of Contrasts in Linear Models,* Vol. 36 (1965), Zentralblatt.

12. International Labour Organization, "KILM 10. Youth Unemployment," 2017, https://www.ilo.org/wcmsp5/groups/public/---dgreports/---stat/documents/publication/wcms_422439.pdf.

13. United Nations Department of Economic and Social Affairs – Youth, n.d., at: https://www.un.org/development/desa/youth/what-we-do/faq.html.

paper uses the African Union definition in the African Youth Charter. The Charter defines youth or young people as every person "between the ages of 15 and 35 years.[14] Since 2013, the ILO has urged countries to use the African Union definition for national statistics and the United Nations definition for international reports.[15] Thus, the Kenya Constitution defines youth as those aged 18 to 35 years. It has been further projected that by 2050, the Africa continent's 18-to-35 demographic will reach more than 800 million.[16] The study is aware of the fact that the youth population is not homogenous, hence the delimitation to Kenyan youth who have graduated from various institutions of higher learning, here referred to as the hustler generation.

In the recent past, humorous images, videos, excerpts of texts, and so on that are copied (often with slight variations) and spread rapidly by internet users have been used by the youth on social media platforms to show their dissatisfaction with the economic regime that perpetuates unemployment and to express their quest for survival. This form of artwork, known as memes, has become a prolific means of communication of the hustler generation's hopes and of resistance. They tend to be light-hearted, often referencing pop culture, usually created anonymously by regular people, and circulated online, yet they are visual arguments that viewers can perceive and that may influence their response to and perception of issues.

Ekdale and Tully observe that in 2010, Kenya's first internet meme arrived in the form of a vigilante named Makmende, the action hero–inspired protagonist of a music video. Within days of the video's release, fans started creating Makmende tales, videos, and artwork and circulating these works online.[17] Ekdale and Tully further note that the participatory playfulness around Makmende created a meme of aspiration through which a niche of Kenyans collectively reimagined a hypermasculine hero who embodied youth's hopes and visions for the country with political and economic stability at home and cultural and technological dominance abroad.[18] From then on, memes have become a popular means through which the youth critique emerging issues in Kenya, albeit with humour and playfulness.

---

14. African Union Commission, African Youth Charter, 2006,
https://au.int/sites/default/files/treaties/7789-treaty-0033_-_african_youth_charter_e.pdf.
15. International Labour Organization, "KILM 10."
16. Hafed Al-Gwhell, "Africa Must Unleash the Potential of Its Growing Youth Population," ARABEWS blog, 12 August 2019, http://www.arabnews.com/node/1495751.
17. Brian Ekdale and Melissa Tully, "Makmende Amerudi: Kenya's Collective Reimagining as a Meme of Aspiration," *Critical Issues in Media Communication* 31: 4 (2014), 283–98.
18. Ibid.

Some of the most popular social media memes among Kenyan youth[19] have been *unafanya hivi … unakufa* (this can be translated as: You innocently take a particular action, but it kills you). Another is: *team ma-hustlers na ma-sufferers* (this can be translated as: We are in the group of those hustling and suffering). The third is: *I may look ok, but deep inside…* and the fourth is: *Niko sawa lakini napambana na hali yangu* (this can be translated as: I am fine, but I am struggling to remain fine). These became so popular that there was a social media push that the fourth one should be made part of the Kenyan national anthem. These memes are short, but they are an expression of the life of youths in the cities. They highlight the challenges and the coping mechanism that youth employ to remain afloat. These selected memes portray a reimagined and redefined symbol of weakness and struggle into symbols of strength, resilience, and willpower to overcome day-to-today hurdles and struggles: the spirit of hustling.

Methodology: Thinking through Mission Praxis

This study uses mission praxis as methodological toolkit in a mainstreaming of youth agenda in a programmatic model. Contextualizing this praxis provides a suitable mark of mission for the church in Kenya, specifically on the concept of mainstreaming of the youth agenda in a programmatic model in seeking justice for the hustler generation. A case study is carried out in the Kenya Anglican Youth Organization (KAYO)'s Green Anglican program as a mission praxis, not only in relation to environmental degradation but also to the graduates' unemployment. The mission praxis cycle was developed and taught at the University of South Africa and concretized in Johannes Zuze Banda's 2010 thesis, "African Renaissance and Missiology: A Perspective from Mission Praxis." Banda shows to what extent faith-based actions contribute to the renaissance debate in Africa.[20] In his thesis, he suggests a missiological perspective as a befitting strand through which the African renaissance can be interrogated and reshaped. He justifies the relevance and legitimacy for missiology in the quest for a new Africa by postulating that missiology is an agent of change, is imminent and is at the core of rebirth, and is itself an advocacy of new life.[21]

---

19. A random Google search shows that in 2018 and 2019, these memes were the most popular: https://www.google.com/search?rlz=1C1VFKB_enKR841KR841&tbm=isch&sa=1&ei=UhqcX MXNMsTn-QaCsKLIDA&q=the+most+popular+whatsapp+memes+2018+in+kenya&oq=the+ most+popular+whatsapp+.

20. Zuze J. Banda, "African Renaissance and Missiology: Perspective from Mission Praxis," PhD diss., University of South Africa, 2010, 101. http://uir.unisa.ac.za/bitstream/ handle/10500/4136/thesis_banda_z.pdf?sequence=1&isAllowed=y.

21. Ibid., 108.

Banda locates this praxis in 1980s, when David Bosch and other professors at the University of South Africa jointly wrote a study guide for the first-level Missiology course there. It has gone through phases of reinterpretation and remodelling, and in 2010 became summarized into a seven-point praxis matrix: spirituality (at the centre), agency, contextual understanding, ecclesial scrutiny, theological interpretation, strategic planning, and reflexivity.[22] Banda uses this praxis to show how the African renaissance can be lived in faith terms and to demonstrate how this matrix can be used in mobilizing a group of committed Christians to work together for transformation in their context; it therefore appeals for the adoption of the matrix as a transformative tool for the call for an African renaissance.[23] This study analyzes the contours of this praxis and shows its milestones as modelled in the KAYO Green Anglican program as a response to graduate (youth) unemployment in Kenya.

Spirituality

In this praxis, spirituality is at the centre of the cycle as a tributary that runs through all other dimensions of the matrix and is based more on the inner voice that feeds convictions and subsequent actions.[24] This proceeds in two strands: a spirituality of right action; and prophetic spirituality. The former is critical and lies at the heart of change in the society, specifically in sociopolitical matters. This type of spirituality is needed to sustain commitment in African faith communities to bring about the desired far-reaching changes that are necessary if any African renaissance is to take place. Prophetic spirituality is linked to the traditional voice of the Old Testament prophets as well as to a spirituality of the cross, which finds its strength in the image of the Suffering Servant, Jesus Christ, and has a dimension of compassion which attempts to meet the needs of the destitute. It therefore confronts the sources of perpetual suffering, addresses root causes of suffering, and digs for answers at the root of the problem.[25] Spirituality as a dimension of the mission praxis entails building convictions – not only with the intention of shaping right action in confronting structural oppressive regimes that perpetuate oppression, but also providing hope in Christ.

---

22. Ibid., 132.
23. Ibid., 131.
24. Ibid.
25. Ibid., 132–37.

Agency

The second dimension is agency: describing individuals and organized groups as instruments of change, especially in sociopolitical matters. In light of missiological application, this is qualified as transformative agency. The role of the church in this dimension is described within two idioms: the five-fold ministry and the priesthood of all believers. As such, the church is an embodiment of power, authority, and service, with the striking element as a missionary agency with an indebtedness to the divine sanctioning. As a transformative agency, the church's two-fold model, corporately or individually, is an enduring agency that exceeds limitations prescribed by human choice, geographic locality, and age. As such, they become strategists who will engage people constructively and increase a sense of dignity and humanity among the poor and the needy without antagonizing the rich and the working class. The church responds here in two ways. First, it shapes those involved to have transformed attitudes and become sensitive to the interests and needs of the people. Second, it participates in the diversified call for agents of change in administering justice and listening to the cry of the marginalized. Third, the church helps communities and individuals formulate problem statements and propose lasting solutions through their writing and conceptual skills. Finally, it creates institutes, produces texts, and introduces mentoring programs, thereby deliberately leaving a trail of a legacy that can be emulated.[26]

Contextual Understanding

The third dimension is contextual understanding. This occurs on two levels: understanding the social space and understanding the physical space. Understanding the social space entails finding and positioning power icons in that space – both those who play positive roles and those who play negative roles – and determining how their existence influences the community. Understanding the physical space involves mapping features in respect to infrastructure and its important role in matters of health, education, and safety. The underlying issue here is to establish how communities are either left vulnerable or enabled against negative forces operating in the community. This helps agents of transformation to understand the dynamics under which they should operate and what types of interventions they need work out using the matrix's different dimensions. The goal in this mapping is for the Christian community to position itself to collaborate with other agencies, since the faith community has established strategies, infrastructure, and personnel, and as such a dynamic force that is already at work in its own way to change communities.[27]

---

26. Ibid., 137–48.
27. Ibid., 149–59.

Ecclesial Scrutiny

The fourth dimension is ecclesial scrutiny. This involves looking at the history of mission and the church in terms of it having a hand in the sociopolitical affairs of the people of Africa and how this involvement had an impact on the quality of life of the people at the grassroots level. The aim is to establish how this history influences the present situation and how it determines the strategy for the way forward.[28]

Theological Interpretation

The fifth dimension is theological interpretation. Here, every intervention strategy must pay attention to emerging theological issues and the impact these issues and forms of doing theology have on the lives of people and their communities and, in particular, on the African people. This leads to theological interpretations which are outcomes-based. Such theologies are not steeped in theories only but find expression in actions, too. This dimension seeks to create theological messages and actions that are sustainable.[29]

Strategic Planning

The sixth dimension in this praxis is strategic planning. It entails planning with a view to effective action and creating synergy between theory and practice.[30]

Reflexivity

The seventh dimension is reflexivity, which is simply an interactive relationship and an interplay of all the dimensions in the missiology matrix. Its purpose is to sharpen the value and the integrity of all the elements of the praxis cycle.[31]

This concretization of missional praxis is important for this study because of its focus and goal. This praxis is aimed at supporting and inspiring the congregation to listen in fresh ways to one another and to the scriptures and then leading them to listen to what is happening among people in their context. It involves the quest for new questions, so that instead of asking how to attract people to what the church is doing, the focus shifts to seeking to understand what God is doing in the neighbourhood and how the church can

28. Ibid., 161.
29. Ibid., 174.
30. Ibid., 184.
31. Ibid., 187.

position herself as an agent of transformation with God in the community where the church finds itself. In this manner, the Anglican Church in Kenya, through mainstreaming the youth agenda as a mark of mission, positions itself as a partner with God in God's activity among the hustlers and with the hustlers in their quest for wholesome growth. KAYO as a department has shifted from offering retention and outreach programs to youth to creating more spaces and platforms for youth for self-development as well as channelling their abilities and energies to generate a positive impact for the community through the Green Anglican movement.

The Mission Praxis of the Green Anglican Movement

Having served as a youth minister in the Anglican Church of Kenya and as a chaplain at St. Paul's University in Machakos, I became part of the historic launch of the Green Anglican movement on 24 October 2018 in my church, All Souls ACK Machakos.[32] This event was spearheaded by the Anglican Students' Fellowship, a group of university students who belong to the Anglican Church of Kenya.[33] This event was attended by youth representatives from all over Kenya as well as environment specialists and representatives from Anglican institutions.

The launch of the Green Anglican movement in Kenya fits into the Anglican Church decade strategy (2018–2027) dubbed "A Wholesome Ministry for a Wholesome Nation." This is specifically part of the tenth pillar, "Wholesome Environment," which focuses on environmental stewardship, awareness, advocacy, clean-up, and adoption of renewable sources of energy.[34] The event, which took one year to plan and to mobilize graduates and students, was a culmination of our two-fold missional strategy for dealing with the challenge of environmental degradation and rampant youth unemployment at the same time. First, our immediate goal was to create hustles for graduates and students by developing a platform and a network where they could creatively and innovatively use the skills they had acquired in school to deal with environmental degradation. Second, our long-term focus was to advocate for recognition, licensing, affirmation, integrating, and harnessing these various youth hustles from the grassroots into the formal and mainstream sector of the country's economy. As an ongoing process, the Green Anglican

---

32. Anglican Church of Kenya, All Souls Machakos Cathedral Youth, "Monthly Report Presented to the Ministries Committee," November 2018.

33. Ibid.

34. Anglican Church of Kenya, "Decade Strategy: 2018–2027," https://issuu.com/anglicaninkenya/docs/ack_decade_strategy_2018-2027.

movement, from conception and now in implementation, employs the mission praxis model as a framework for executing our missional mandate.

Spirituality and Transformation Agency

The first symmetry of the seven-point matrix in the Green Anglican movement is on spirituality and transformation agency. The former entails building convictions with the aim of not only shaping right action but also providing hope in Christ.[35] The latter (as a missional approach) entails shaping those with a role to play to have transformed attitudes and to participate in the diversified call for agents of change in society.[36] The key activity here is mentoring, which is the main platform and which takes two trajectories: professional mentoring and spiritual mentoring.[37] Under spiritual mentoring, the main agenda is to tailor discipleship training and programs targeting young people in schools, neighbourhoods, and workplaces. The tasks include creating Green Anglican groups and small fellowships on campuses, in neighbourhoods, and in workplaces and linking young people to older faithful volunteers for mentoring relationships that can be tracked, monitored, evaluated, and reported.[38] Under professional mentoring, the main agenda is two-fold. The first step is to create a database of available and reachable Christian professionals who are willing to "adopt" small groups or individual young people and walk with them through life decisions (in their career, relationships, and finances) using faith as the decision-making tool.[39] This "adoption" relationship is also tracked, monitored, evaluated, and reported. The second step is to mobilize young professionals (and older ones as well) who are church "alumni" (such as KAYO alumni) to initiate creative ways of doing ministry within the church and reaching out to the community.[40]

Contextual Understanding, Ecclesial Scrutiny, and Theological Interpretation

The second symmetry is on contextual understanding, ecclesial scrutiny, and theological interpretation. The aim is to construct theologies which are not steeped in theories only but find expression in actions that are

---

35. Anglican Students Fellowship, "Green Anglican Movement Concept Paper" (2018),.3.
36. Ibid.
37. Ibid.
38. Ibid., 4.
39. Ibid., 5.
40. Ibid.

sustainable.[41] It begins with a critical appraisal of intervention strategies which pay attention to emerging theological issues and the consequent impact these issues and forms of doing theology have on the lives of people and their communities. The theological rationale of this project is hinged on the concept of responsible stewardship. This is a critique of both an exploitative dominion-orientated attitude toward creation and the intricate nexus of corruption with impunity and political patronage, a combination which is the greatest impediment to national and global economic progress. The two major activities carried out at this level are contextual Bible studies in universities[42] and advocacy at national level.[43] Through creatively developed manuals and study materials, the Green Anglican movement has created Anglican student fellowships in universities, where creative ways of imagining stewardship emerge from open group discussions and Bible study. When it comes to advocacy, the KAYO movement is at the forefront in supporting the archbishop's call for the church to stop sanitizing graft proceeds of corruption and money laundering through church fundraisers and handouts. The aim is to inculcate the virtue of hard work (with the mantra "dirty hands make clean money") and to raise young people with integrity who can challenge all forms of corruption at the grassroots level.

Strategic Planning and Reflexivity

The third symmetry is on strategic planning and reflexivity. This involves creating synergy between theory and practice and sharpening the value and integrity of all the elements of the praxis cycle for effective action. This approach provides a sense of direction and outlines measurable goals, guiding day-to-day decisions, evaluating progress, and changing approaches when moving forward. Through this, the movement has come up with strategic objectives which are backed up with realistic, thoroughly researched, and quantifiable benchmarks for evaluating results.[44] The five-year strategic plan, dubbed "Integrity of Creation and Justice for the Youth," which hinges on the Anglican Church of Kenya Decade plan, focuses on three things: capacity building, community mobilization, and partnerships.[45] On capacity building, the movement envisions training 10,000 youth (including trainers of trainers) on environmental conservation within five years. Key areas of focus include

---

41. Ibid., 8.

42. *Anglican Students Fellowship Study Guide* (Nairobi: Uzima Publishers, 2018).

43. Anglican Church of Kenya, "Decade Strategy: 2018–2027."

44. Anglican Students' Fellowship, "Green Anglican Strategic Plan: 2018–2022."

45. Ibid.

adopting ozone- and climate-friendly technologies and finding creative ways to conserve the environment and to repair damage and reverse trends.[46] This has the potential of creating new hustles for youth. On community mobilization, the movement envisions rallying the community in adopting climate-friendly technologies and care for the earth. Social media, artwork, and music are key platforms for the campaign.[47] On partnerships, the movement envisions reaching out to various stakeholders in the public and private sectors on advocacy matters and involving youth and youth groups in policy making and implementation with the aim of broadening the space for job creation and opportunities for new hustles.[48]

Conclusion

This study has taken the case of mission praxis of the Green Anglican movement in Kenya, especially its specific activities within the KAYO, an Anglican youth organization. It has explored this using a symmetrical approach of the mission praxis seven-point matrix: spirituality, transformation agency, contextual understanding, ecclesial scrutiny, theological interpretation, strategic planning, and reflexivity. In so doing, the study has shown the role the church can play in dealing with unemployment in Kenya. The church has a two-fold role in this venture. The first is in creating hustles for graduates, and the second is in advocating for the licensing, affirmation, integrating, and harnessing of various youth hustles into the formal sector of the economy. This will ensure job security and guarantee social benefits like health insurance and social security for youth. This is what the study calls the mainstreaming of the youth agenda in a programmatic model: the case of the Anglican Church of Kenya through the KAYO Green Anglican movement.

The underlying factor for which the study proposes this response is the tendency and risk to unjustly regard hustling as an exoneration of formal employment policies that place the burden of job creation on the shoulders of young people themselves. While hustling may be regarded as graduates struggling against adversity, more than anything else it is a clear indication of the failure of the state to uphold its end of the intergenerational bargain. The church can therefore be an affirming space for hustlers and restore hope and dignity for many of them in Kenya. It is a holistic approach for a wholesome ministry for a wholesome nation.

------

46. Ibid.
47. Ibid.
48. Ibid.

6

Terre et déplacement (justice économique, justice écologique et migration)

Grâce Pericles Mongo-Bouya

Résumé

Absence de travail, apparition de conflits, manque de logements, insécurité alimentaire, dégradation des terres, marginalisation des jeunes, absence de justice économique et environnementale… Tous ces phénomènes entraînent divers déplacements au niveau continental. L'objectif de ce travail est d'identifier les problèmes liés aux déplacements qui sont dus à l'injustice (économique, écologique) pour lutter contre la migration. De manière spécifique, il s'agit de proposer des mécanismes permettant à l'Église de s'engager avec fermeté dans un plaidoyer contre l'injustice et la migration. En effet, il est important de mettre en place une loi qui permet aux victimes d'injustices de dénoncer leur situation et d'obtenir d'éventuelles réparations.

Introduction

Le monde est en perpétuelle mutation et l'Église ne peut rester en marge de toutes ces évolutions. En leur qualité de garants des institutions au niveau continental et national, les chefs d'État et de gouvernement doivent prendre conscience de ces faits. Quant aux responsables des Églises, ils doivent refléter le modèle du Christ, Bon Berger. À ce titre, il leur revient de s'occuper de la vie aussi bien morale, éthique et matérielle que spirituelle des fidèles – des fidèles qui représentent une part importante de la population mondiale et qui peuvent influencer les valeurs de qualité de leur société.

Cependant, beaucoup de jeunes et de femmes, dans le monde en général et en Afrique en particulier, sont marginalisés. Dans plusieurs domaines (éducation, justice, santé, environnement, et économie), ils continuent d'être à la traîne en matière de leadership et d'exercice de leurs droits. Face à cette situation, il est impérieux que l'Église aide les femmes et les jeunes. Comment? En intériorisant les principes des objectifs du développement durable qui permettent de réduire les inégalités constatées en matière de justice et de paix, et en favorisant un plaidoyer pour la justice et l'immigration de la population africaine, et des jeunes en particulier.

En effet, les estimations montrent que l'Afrique en 2063 sera le continent le plus peuplé du monde[1]. Elle aura la plus grande proportion de jeunes, dont 70% ou plus seront hautement qualifiés. De surcroît, le continent enregistrera le pourcentage le plus élevé de citoyens et citoyennes de classe moyenne disposant d'un pouvoir d'achat important.

On ne peut pas ignorer que l'un des facteurs clés de la prospérité de l'Afrique tiendra à son capital humain d'envergure mondiale. Et un développement de celui-ci est prévisible, grâce à une éducation de qualité axée sur l'atteinte d'un pourcentage de 100% en lecture, calcul et écriture. Un tel développement mettra l'accent sur la science, la technologie et l'ingénierie. De plus, l'accès universel à une éducation de qualité et à des programmes de formation accrédités à tous les niveaux sera inscrit dans la loi à l'horizon 2063.

Malgré ces projections, de nos jours, l'Afrique connaît un grand retard en matière de développement. Cela est dû aux conflits internes, entre peuples par exemple, qui dégénèrent en guerres civiles. Et leur principale cause reste l'exploitation illicite et sous la contrainte des ressources naturelles. C'est le cas au Nord-Kivu, en République démocratique du Congo (RDC), par exemple. Ces conflits sont à l'origine des déplacements divers des populations vers d'autres horizons.

D'autres éléments sont à prendre en ligne de compte comme facteurs de ces déplacements: les conditions de vie précaire, la famine, la pauvreté, le sous-emploi, la marginalisation des jeunes par la vieille classe politique…

Sur ce sujet, les jeunes ne peuvent pas s'exprimer: leur recherche du bonheur les place dans une situation difficile. Ils s'exposent aux déplacements, parfois sous la contrainte, et quittent leur terre pour trouver refuge dans des pays jugés meilleurs que le leur, car offrant des conditions de vie indispensables, comme l'accès à des soins de santé de qualité et à l'emploi. Et où ils supposent possible de s'exprimer et de faire valoir leurs idées et savoir-faire. C'est là l'une des causes de la migration et de l'injustice écologique et économique, partagées par le commun de mortel, lorsque l'environnement ne leur permet pas de faire valoir leurs compétences et de bénéficier d'une qualité de vie propice. Cela s'explique par l'absence d'une justice équitable sur le continent.

S'il s'agit vraiment d'un choix, le choix de ce thème se justifie par l'intérêt que nous accordons au développement de notre continent à travers sa jeunesse, car elle représente une force motrice tout à fait capable d'apporter le changement et de rendre l'Afrique émergente d'ici 2063, ce qui est « l'Afrique

---

1. Agenda 2063.

que nous voulons », en apportant des changements sur le plan culturel et sur le plan éducatif, en exploitant de nouvelles opportunités, en mettant l'accent sur la technologie, etc. Ce qui va nous interpeller, nous Corps du Christ, nous incitant à revisiter les besoins les plus pressants dans leurs contextes particuliers, à réfléchir à ces différents besoins en vue de mettre en place les valeurs évangéliques et d'agir concrètement avec d'autres acteurs pour l'intérêt commun de notre humanité.

Au-delà de ces faits, il est important que l'Afrique se lève ensemble avec sa jeunesse. Avec elle, elle partagera une même vision d'une Afrique unie et inséparable. Et réconciliées, toutes deux œuvreront à trouver des pistes pour éradiquer le phénomène d'immigration. Et toutes deux plaideront contre l'injustice tant économique qu'écologique, se montrant équitables à l'égard des hommes, des femmes et des jeunes vivant sur le continent. C'est pour cela que les autorités gouvernementales et les institutions, ainsi que les mouvements sociaux et religieux, se sont accordées pour mettre en place l'Agenda 2063, avec pour slogan « l'Afrique que nous voulons ». L'Agenda 2063 énonce quelques aspirations[2] pour mettre fin aux différentes inégalités constatées. Ces aspirations viennent du fait que la population africaine de diverses origines sociales et de la diaspora a accepté la vision de l'Union africaine (UA) de construire une « *Afrique intégrée, prospère et pacifique, dirigée par ses propres citoyens, et représentant une force dynamique sur la scène mondiale* ».

Cet Agenda représente le guide fondamental pour l'avenir du continent africain. Mais il ne doit pas être un simple texte, il nous faut plutôt le mettre en pratique pour que « l'Afrique que nous voulons » devienne réalité et ne reste pas un slogan vide. Cela met l'accent sur la qualité de vie, l'égalité de tous les êtres humains et une justice économique et écologique équitable, qui contribuerait à la lutte contre la migration illégale de la population africaine vers l'Orient.

Ces aspirations conduisent d'une part à:
- Une Afrique prospère, fondée sur une croissance inclusive et un développement durable;
- Une Afrique où règnent la bonne gouvernance, la démocratie, le respect des droits de l'homme, la justice et l'état de droit;
- Une Afrique dont le développement est axé sur ses citoyennes et citoyens, puisant dans le potentiel de ses populations, en particulier de ses femmes et de ses jeunes, et prenant soin de ses enfants.

---

2. Cadre de l'Agenda 2063, l'Afrique que nous voulons.

D'autre part, ces aspirations conduisent à un continent qui intègre avant tout des processus d'adaptation pour maintenir des écosystèmes sains et préserver l'environnement naturel de l'Afrique, plus grande réserve restante d'eaux cristallines, de forêts anciennes et de terres dans le monde.

Enfin, ces aspirations conduisent à des économies structurellement transformées pour stimuler la croissance grâce à l'entrepreneuriat et créer des emplois décents pour tous et toutes.

L'objectif est que, d'ici à 2063, les pays africains affichent des indicateurs de qualité de la vie parmi les plus performants au monde. D'où l'intérêt pour l'Église de s'investir en ce sens en tant que partenaire efficace du développement.

Après cet aperçu, la question qui se pose à nous est de savoir ce que nous faisons du constat que l'Afrique compte des pays avec une croissance économique parmi les plus rapides au monde. Ne voyons-nous pas que le développement social est également extraordinaire en Afrique, et que la majorité de la population a accès à l'éducation, à la santé, à la communication, aux services financiers, etc. ?

L'Afrique a une Église dynamique. Et la foi a toujours de l'importance pour les peuples, même si elle est parfois une cause majeure de conflits, comme dans le monde entier. Comme l'a affirmé le pasteur Fidon Mwombeki secrétaire général de la Conférence des Églises de toute l'Afrique (CETA), lors de son discours introductif à la 11ᵉ assemblée générale organisée à Kigali:

> *L'Afrique est un continent en croissance. Telle est ma perception du continent, et c'est pour cela que je viens au service de l'Église en Afrique.*

J'inscris ma réflexion dans la lignée de ces propos. Je partage cet avis. En effet, dans le monde entier, des États-Unis à l'Europe, si ces pays ont accédé vite au développement c'est grâce aux peuples africains et à leur richesse. Grâce à nos ressources naturelles renouvelables ou non renouvelables, l'Occident a connu la révolution industrielle, transformant les matières premières en produits manufacturés.

Ceci doit interpeller la conscience de la jeunesse africaine et l'inciter à prendre en main son destin. J'insiste, car le développement de l'Afrique en dépend. L'unité et le dynamisme de la jeunesse africaine entraîneront son développement tant attendu par nos prédécesseurs qui ont lancé le panafricanisme.

La CETA et le COE qui s'offrent à nous sont des instruments des Églises en Afrique. Ce sont des organisations œcuméniques fortes, avec une présence et une portée continentales. Par ailleurs, elles ont un bon leadership et un héritage établi.

D'où l'importance que nous accordons à ce thème « Terre et déplacement ». C'est une cause particulière de la marche vers la migration qui touche profondément la jeunesse africaine. Elle peut venir de l'injustice non seulement économique, mais aussi écologique.

Nous avons besoin de l'accompagnement de Dieu tout au long de ce plaidoyer pour la mise en place d'une justice équitable pour toutes et tous et pour lutter contre la migration illégale des jeunes Africains et Africaines.

En effet, nous croyons que la prière nous aidera à atteindre cet objectif de « l'Afrique que nous voulons » d'ici à 2063. Ce thème a pour objectif général d'identifier les problèmes liés aux déplacements dus à la justice économique et écologique et de lutter contre la migration. Spécifiquement, il s'agit de proposer des mécanismes permettant à l'Église et aux confessions œcuméniques de s'engager avec fermeté dans un plaidoyer contre l'injustice et la migration, pour le progrès du peuple de Dieu et l'Afrique en général.

Cet objectif veut nous amener à des mécanismes qui permettront de rendre équitable la justice économique et écologique, dans le but de lutter contre la migration dans le contexte africain.

Ainsi cet objectif contribuera-t-il à faire des hommes, des femmes et des jeunes des acteurs dynamiques du développement faisant preuve de créativité pour réduire les inégalités enfreignant la justice et provoquant la migration. Car le Dieu de vie nous amènera à être des instruments vivants de justice et de paix dans notre lutte contre le déplacement des jeunes vers l'Occident. En effet, le développement de l'Afrique est tributaire de leurs apports. Et leur destinée n'est pas de périr en Méditerranée, mais plutôt de vivre pour une Afrique dynamique, solidaire et patriote. Comme la Bible le déclare dans Deutéronome 1,16 : « *Alors j'ai donné des ordres à vos juges : "Vous entendrez les causes de vos frères, et vous trancherez avec justice les affaires de chacun avec son frère, ou avec l'émigré qu'il a chez lui."* »

Dans la suite, nous allons développer dans un premier temps la justice, deuxièmement la migration, et enfin proposer des pistes de solution.

Justice économique et écologique et migration

Justice économique et écologique

Aujourd'hui, les États africains doivent se fixer pour objectif d'atteindre un développement durable et équitable qui nécessite, entre autres, une justice efficace et une paix effective. Cette justice doit reposer sur l'état de droit effectif, un exercice effectif des droits à la justice, le renforcement de l'égalité et l'équité de tous les citoyens et citoyennes.

Justice écologique

Lorsqu'il s'agit d'accéder à un cadre de vie de qualité, de se prémunir contre certains risques, d'accéder à des ressources naturelles essentielles comme l'eau, l'énergie, le poisson par la pêche et les animaux par la chasse, et d'autre part de participer à la réduction de notre empreinte écologique, les enjeux environnementaux apparaissent de plus en plus comme de nouveaux facteurs d'inégalité potentiels. En effet, il faut connaître la réalité d'aujourd'hui pour s'engager avec fermeté dans un plaidoyer contre l'injustice écologique au service du développement du peuple de Dieu et de l'Afrique en particulier.

Dans les pays développés comme dans les pays en développement, la justice écologique est devenue l'une des priorités des États et des gouvernements pour préserver l'environnement et offrir aux populations une qualité de vie plus saine. C'est la raison pour laquelle la communauté internationale, lors des COP (21, 22, etc.) et d'autres sommets organisés à l'international par les Nations Unies, permet aujourd'hui de prendre des lois, décrets et arrêtés pour préserver les ressources naturelles et interdire la déforestation illégale de la flore et de la faune par des actions humaines ainsi que les actions toxiques des industries qui polluent l'eau en recyclant leurs matériaux et produits, etc.

En outre, les déplacements humains vers d'autres continents et d'autres pays mettent en péril la survie de l'écosystème et de la biodiversité. Par exemple, certaines personnes émigrent vers d'autres horizons pour exercer des activités comme la cueillette, la chasse, la pêche, la transformation du bois en charbon (coupe des arbres), l'exploitation minière, pour ne citer que celles-là. Ce qui met en péril la survie de l'environnement. Et cela crée des externalités négatives au sein de l'environnement lorsque ces activités ne sont pas régies par des lois ou sont exercées de façon illicite. De ce fait, il est important de mettre en place une réglementation rigoureuse portant sur la préservation de l'environnement. Au Congo, par exemple, il existe une loi dans ce domaine, datant de 1991 (loi n° 003/91 du 23 avril 1991).

En effet, toute personne (ressortissante ou étrangère) résidant dans un pays doit prendre connaissance des différents lois et décrets en vigueur et apprendre à s'y conformer. Le non-respect et l'exercice illicite des activités entraînent des sanctions. Au Congo, par exemple, des citoyens et des étrangers continuent de pratiquer la chasse illicitement pendant la période de fermeture. Lorsqu'ils sont rattrapés par les agents de l'ordre, ils subissent les dispositions prévues par la loi.

Ensuite, les corporations industrielles qui exploitent les ressources naturelles du continent, notamment minières et pétrolières, fragilisent dangereusement la vie des populations – en raison de la pollution de l'eau et de l'air, de la dégradation de l'environnement (sécheresse, érosion) – lorsqu'elles ne prennent pas en considération l'impact que ces activités peuvent causer sur l'environnement et la santé humaine[3].

Enfin, la question qui se pose avec acuité est de savoir de quels outils nous disposons aujourd'hui pour lutter contre ces inégalités potentielles et pour construire une nouvelle forme de solidarité écologique.

Il ressort de ce qui précède que les solutions proposées en matière de solidarité environnementale sont liées aux cultures politiques des pays qui les instituent. Au-delà des lois existantes sur la protection de l'environnement en Afrique, il nous faut créer une loi permettant aux victimes d'injustices de dénoncer leur situation et d'obtenir d'éventuelles réparations. Prenons par exemple le cas des pays anglo-saxons: ils ont développé une approche de la justice environnementale passant par l'institution d'une loi. De plus, l'action publique doit permettre de corriger les inégalités environnementales en s'attaquant aux mécanismes qui produisent ces inégalités. En revanche, quelques pays d'Europe continentale utilisent une approche plus interventionniste[4]. Comme l'indiquent Laigle et Tual, il faudra que les États puissent mettre en œuvre une charte environnementale pour que toutes les sociétés exerçant à l'échelle continentale assument la responsabilité des dommages qu'elles causent.

En somme, la justice écologique ne doit faire d'exception pour personne, qu'il s'agisse de personnes physiques ou morales.

---

3. Ceci fait appel à la responsabilité sociétale des entreprises: elles doivent intégrer volontairement dans leurs activités les principes du développement durable.

4. Cf. Laigle et Tual, qui développent la théorie interventionniste de l'environnement.

Justice économique

L'injustice sociale est devenue une préoccupation politique majeure au fil de la crise économique. Les politiques sociales jouent donc un rôle essentiel non seulement en faisant reculer la pauvreté, mais encore en favorisant le développement économique et l'intégration sociale.

Force est de constater, au niveau mondial, la stagnation des salaires d'une grande majorité de la population d'un côté et l'augmentation de la fortune d'un petit nombre de l'autre. L'injustice économique grandit, en particulier en Afrique. Il est nécessaire de faire ressortir quelques éléments permettant d'envisager des mesures propices à un avenir heureux et de lutter contre ces injustices économiques constatées. Certes, une bonne partie des hommes et des femmes détenant le pouvoir de l'État sont plus riches que leurs populations, en raison du détournement des deniers publics à leur propre compte. Ces personnes engrangent des sommes colossales au détriment du bien-être collectif. Quant à la redistribution de la richesse nationale, elle pose encore un réel problème en Afrique, car dans la plupart des pays en développement, par exemple dans la région centrale, les ressources sont vendues au profit des politiques, qui sont trente fois plus riches que les hommes et femmes d'affaires. Cela est imputable aux nombreux détournements des fonds publics destinés à des programmes d'intérêt public qui auraient dû renforcer l'emploi et le développement des infrastructures de base dans des secteurs comme l'éducation, la santé, les routes, l'énergie, etc.

Une attention insuffisante portée à ces fonctions générales de la politique économique peut menacer les progrès d'autres objectifs du développement, en suscitant des tensions sociales du fait de la rareté des ressources, en compromettant la santé et la productivité ou en empêchant d'investir dans les générations futures. Dans le pire des cas, ces échecs peuvent entraîner un conflit violent ou une nouvelle dégradation de l'environnement.

En effet, plusieurs inégalités sont observées au niveau du commerce, des échanges et l'emploi des jeunes. Le cadre commercial d'autres pays repose sur des lois qui régissent l'exercice de certaines activités, ce qui rend quelques réformes nécessaires. Au Bénin, par exemple, les étrangers n'ont pas le droit de commercer, tandis qu'au Congo bon nombre de Béninois et Béninoises font du commerce. Autre problème, le chômage augmente du fait que les classes plus âgées ne donnent pas aux jeunes la possibilité de travailler. Par exemple, au Congo, plusieurs générations sont livrées au chômage en raison des classes âgées qui se maintiennent à des postes à responsabilités, notamment à certains échelons et dans les institutions habilitées à promulguer les lois qui régissent la vie de la nation. En outre, les pensions de retraite deviennent un casse-tête au Congo lorsqu'elles restent impayées pendant 7 à 12 mois. Une majorité des personnes percevant une retraite ont pourtant des problèmes de santé qui leur coûtent très cher. Comment évoluera le sort des jeunes et des personnes retraitées si la situation n'est pas résolue d'ici peu?

Enfin, il est important de corriger les disparités flagrantes de revenu ou de bien-être et de garantir un niveau d'égalité socialement acceptable par des interventions sociales directes ou par la gestion des effets distributifs d'autres politiques économiques.

En résumé, il faut une justice économique véritable qui puisse contenter l'ensemble des ressortissants et ressortissantes d'un pays.

Migration

Le niveau exceptionnellement élevé de migration est lié aux inégalités économiques, aux troubles politiques, aux conflits et aux dégradations de l'environnement, mais une grande partie tient davantage à l'histoire commune que partagent de nombreuses populations de la région. Du fait de cette histoire commune, les frontières entre la plupart des pays de la région sont assez poreuses, voire carrément ouvertes dans certains cas. C'est le cas, par exemple, de l'Afrique centrale, où la RDC, le Congo, le Rwanda, l'Ouganda, l'Angola, le Gabon, le Cameroun et la République centrafricaine, pour ne citer que ces pays-là, sombrent dans le ventre mou des problèmes à rebondissements. Cela facilite évidemment les migrations intrarégionales, même s'il existe aussi une migration vers l'Europe dans des conditions parfois très dangereuses.

Il est important pour nous de constituer un espace politique relativement unifié au sein de la communauté africaine. Pour stimuler la création d'un espace économique commun et pour aménager nos conditions de vie en mettant en place des politiques de développement durable axées sur ces trois piliers: économie, environnement et social.

La migration est l'une des causes qui freinent le développement du continent africain. Les États africains ont mis en place plusieurs politiques pour le bien-être de leurs compatriotes. Malgré cela, il n'y a pas eu de concrétisation. L'Afrique est plongée dans les conflits d'intérêts (guerre civile, rébellions, etc.) et, par ailleurs, elle souffre du manque de politiques adéquates facilitant l'accès à un travail de qualité pour les jeunes et du manque d'infrastructures de santé, d'éducation et de promotion de l'entrepreneuriat. Cette situation pousse les jeunes à migrer vers d'autres terres qu'ils ou elles croient en paix, dotées d'une justice équitable et leur permettant de travailler dans un cadre favorable.

À vrai dire, le problème de la migration représente une perte en matière de capital humain. Aujourd'hui, le phénomène de la fuite des cerveaux reste une question importante. Il constitue un problème crucial pour nos pays d'origine, dans la mesure où il entrave le développement local au bénéfice des économies européennes. Il faut de toute évidence mettre en place une vision unique sur le continent pour lutter contre la migration. Parce que le départ des jeunes vers d'autres horizons constitue une perte pour l'avenir du continent.

Il nous faut prendre des mesures salutaires afin que des politiques adéquates soient mises en œuvre pour assurer un lendemain meilleur. Par ailleurs, au niveau régional, la majeure partie des jeunes quitte les campagnes pour chercher du travail en ville. Cela a un impact sur l'économie nationale, parce que les jeunes devraient exploiter des terres riches pour développer l'agriculture. Tel n'est pas le cas, puisqu'on les voit migrer vers d'autres sols, d'autres *terres*. Par voie de conséquence, les États doivent mettre en place des politiques adaptées à chaque secteur en vue de promouvoir le développement et de stabiliser l'emploi non seulement des jeunes, mais aussi des générations futures.

Plusieurs exemples peuvent appuyer notre thèse sur les différentes causes de la migration au niveau continental. Ainsi, au Soudan, la population considère encore la migration comme une expérience temporaire visant à améliorer ses connaissances et ses revenus. Sur ce point, les statistiques fournies par les autorités d'Arabie saoudite montrent qu'environ 500 000 ressortissantes et ressortissants soudanais étaient enregistrés dans ce pays en mai 2008, dont 54,1% d'hommes, et 27,1% de personnes émigrées qui travaillent. En effet, selon les rapports du gouvernement, le pays a subi un départ massif de travailleurs et travailleuses qualifiés, notamment de médecins, dont le nombre ne cesse de croître.

Aujourd'hui, l'Afrique du Nord est considérée au sud du Sahara comme une porte d'entrée vers l'Europe. Devant les difficultés apparentes et l'impossibilité, la plupart du temps, d'obtenir un visa pour entrer légalement en Europe, cette région devient un passage obligé pour les candidats et candidates à la migration d'Afrique subsaharienne qui veulent entrer en

Europe du Sud, via les enclaves espagnoles de Ceuta et Melilla ou via l'Italie.

En réalité, cette migration présente les caractéristiques générales suivantes: concernant au départ des hommes, elle s'est féminisée et touche désormais aussi des enfants. L'âge moyen est de 27 ans. Les mineurs non accompagnés qui tentent également l'aventure ont entre 15 et 17 ans. Le nombre de femmes accompagnées de bébés est en nette augmentation. Généralement, les femmes entament leur migration seules, mais elles enfantent au cours de leur migration, soit à la suite d'un viol ou de l'exploitation sexuelle, soit à la suite de leur vie en concubinage (qui constitue surtout une protection, rarement une vie de couple). D'autre part, les personnes qui réussissent à migrer aboutissent parfois, faute de papiers, dans des groupes terroristes, se livrent à la vente de drogue, et voient leur destin désorienté.

Il est important pour chaque État de mener des études sur la migration afin de collecter des données sur leur diaspora et sur son rôle potentiel dans le développement de nos États. Car l'avenir de l'Afrique dépend de l'implication de ces citoyennes et citoyens; personne d'autre ne peut développer l'Afrique. Seuls la conscience des jeunes et leur dynamisme apporteront le changement sur notre continent. Il est important de souligner le rôle des États, qui doivent s'impliquer dans les politiques de développement pour lutter contre ce fléau qui détruit la jeunesse africaine. C'est là qu'intervient l'importance des Églises et du mouvement œcuménique, qui doivent mener des plaidoyers et s'organiser sur les thématiques de la paix et de la justice pour convaincre les instances de décision d'investir dans ce processus.

En définitive, la migration est un mal nécessaire. À nous de prendre conscience de son ampleur sur toutes ces facettes.

Pistes de solutions et perspective de l'Église évangélique du Congo (EEC)

Perspectives

L'Église évangélique du Congo (EEC), membre de la CETA et du COE, n'est pas restée à la marge face à cette thématique qui est devenue la priorité du Corps de Christ. Nous pouvons citer quelques-unes des actions réalisées récemment:

- Tous les 5 juin, l'EEC organise des thèmes sur justice et paix pour lutter contre l'injustice (sociale, économique, écologique, raciale) au Congo. Un département est chargé de s'occuper de ces questions: l'AEP (Action évangélique pour la paix), qui dispose de cellules au niveau de nos paroisses.

- En 2018, l'EEC a aidé des personnes déplacées dans le département du Pool, au sud du pays. Leur migration était occasionnée par la rébellion organisée par le pasteur Frederick Missamou alias Ntoumi. Les paroisses ont constitué des lieux d'accueil de ces personnes.
- Sur les questions du genre, des violences sont observées dans la société congolaise, et l'EEC n'est pas épargnée. C'est pour cela que des campagnes de sensibilisation ont été menées dans tous les consistoires évangéliques, à savoir dans les paroisses urbaines et rurales, du 22 au 24 novembre 2018. Elles avaient pour thème « L'EEC et la lutte contre les violences basées sur le genre en son sein et dans les familles » et s'appuyaient sur 2 Pierre 1,6.

Pistes de solutions

Partant de ce qui précède, nous formulons quelques recommandations.

La justice économique et écologique, entre autres, incite les êtres humains à la migration. Cependant, le développement des pays africains permettrait d'éviter les drames auxquels nous assistons de nos jours. Pour ce faire:

- Les États doivent améliorer la gouvernance de façon à associer les jeunes dans la définition des politiques publiques, des lois et dans l'élaboration des projets de développement.
- Une loi commune sur la préservation de l'environnement doit être mise en place au niveau continental.
- Une bonne gouvernance des fonds publics destinés à la santé, à l'éducation, à l'emploi des jeunes et à la préservation de l'environnement permettra l'intégration économique des pays africains.
- L'Église doit employer des dispositifs de sensibilisation pour aider les populations à mieux connaître leurs droits. Cette ignorance a contribué à l'apparition d'un grand nombre de migrants et migrantes en situation irrégulière dans la région.
- Il est important de favoriser l'accès aux services de base au niveau continental, en encourageant le passage de structures informelles à des structures formelles dans les programmes visant à financer les jeunes désirant entreprendre.
- L'éducation et la Parole de Dieu doivent être considérées comme

des éléments clés de la stratégie de communication en matière de migration.

- L'Église doit élaborer des messages cohérents et doit se coordonner pour communiquer sur les initiatives et politiques migratoires, dans le but de renforcer la crédibilité des messages.

Conclusion

En guise de conclusion, l'Afrique doit adopter une attitude lucide et responsable, pour protéger ses citoyennes et citoyens victimes de l'injustice tant économique qu'écologique en mettant en place des lois et règlements dans différents secteurs de l'activité économique. Cela vise à encourager l'emploi des jeunes et les activités qui permettent de créer la richesse au niveau continental. Pour rendre l'agenda 2063 effectif, les États doivent avoir les mêmes visions et priorités en matière de développement. L'Afrique doit impulser sa propre politique et définir ses priorités en matière de santé, d'éducation, d'emploi et de préservation de l'environnement. La migration étant un fait social multidimensionnel, elle doit être traitée dans sa globalité et sous toutes ses facettes. Enfin, l'Église doit désormais jouer son rôle prophétique pour une justice et une paix durable et inclusive dans nos communautés et au niveau continental, pour le bien-être de toute la population africaine.

A Rereading of 1 Timothy 2:12 for Gender Justice in the Evangelical Church Winning All

Moses Iliya Ogidis

Abstract

The Evangelical Church Winning All (ECWA) in Nigeria has used 1 Timothy 2:12 as a basis to enshrine in its constitution that women are not to be ordained. Even though the church is aware of ongoing conversations on gender justice, the position of women has mainly remained in the women's fellowship. Since, according to ECWA interpretation, the status quo gets support from the Bible, which ECWA regards as inspired, women continue to be subjected to injustices with regard to their participation in leadership. This essay offers a rereading of 1 Timothy 2:12 toward gender justice in view of the subjugation of women described above.

Introduction

I was brought up in the Evangelical Church Winning All (ECWA) in Nigeria. My theological education did not challenge my position and that of the church on women's ordination and ministry. I applied for postgraduate studies at St. Paul's University in Limuru, Kenya. My first shock was in attending a community service and finding an ordained woman from the Anglican Church leading the service and being a celebrant of holy communion. I later learned that she was the second woman to be ordained in the Anglican Church of Kenya and was a lecturer in church history in the Faculty of Theology. My struggle in the service was whether I should partake of holy communion. My church did not allow women to be ordained, and I have held my church's teaching with high esteem; I am a minister myself. In the end, I did not participate in holy communion because it was celebrated by a woman.

I started my theology course and began interacting with different scholars. I noted that some scholars have engaged with the issue of women and the church, especially African women scholars. In the history of the growth of the church, there have been disparities between men and women,[1] such as

---

1. Mercy Amba Oduyoye and Musimbi R.A. Kanyoro, eds, *The Will to Arise: Women, Tradition,*

subjecting women to the leadership of men and denying the fact that women can also be called by God into ordained ministry.

In some courses, I was challenged with new ways of reading the Bible, especially the Pauline injunctions on women in the church. This was the beginning of my journey on the ordination of women in my church. Some of the methods I was exposed to included new ways of reading the Bible through narratives. A method that is popular with African women theologians is the Circle of Concerned Women Theologians, popularly known as "the Circle." In my Bible, history, and theology classes, I was challenged to use women as one of my lenses to study theology; I was introduced to the readings of the Circle, especially biblical scholars like Teresa Okure, Musa Dube, and postcolonial feminist hermeneutics. This exposure led me to start thinking about my context and that of ECWA and other churches that object to the ordination of women. I realized that one of the leading reasons is Paul's injunctions, especially in 1 Timothy 2:12.

This essay is divided into three sections. It begins with an elucidation of ECWA and the role of women. The next section is a rereading of 1 Timothy 2:12. Finally, the third section envisions gender justice in the ECWA.

The Evangelical Church Winning All and the Role of Women

ECWA is one of the fastest-growing Christian denominations in Nigeria, with over ten million members spread over the entire world. ECWA was formally known as the Association of Evangelical Churches of West Africa and later the Evangelical Church of West Africa. It is built on the foundation of the Sudan Interior Mission (SIM), now called Serving In Mission. SIM came into being because of the vision of a godly mother, Mrs Gowans. Walter Gowans, the son of Mrs Gowans, was the leader of the three pioneer missionaries of SIM. His two other missionary companions were Thomas Kent and Rowland Bingham.[2] Even though they knew that this venture could lead to the loss of their lives, they determined to risk it in faith. Their sacrifice gave birth to ECWA. The goal of ECWA, as stated in the *Minister's Handbook*, is to glorify God.[3] It is my argument that glorifying God means fully including women who are called into the ministry of the word and sacraments by ordaining them, too.

---

and the Church in Africa (Maryknoll: Orbis, 1992), 140.

2. Olatayo, 1999.

3. ECWA Minister's Handbook (Jos: ECWA Headquarters, 2002), iv.

In ECWA, the majority of members are women. They are instrumental in supporting the ordained ministers, especially their wives. However, the role of women is restricted to the women's fellowship and includes singing, hospitality, cleaning the church, prayers, serving as Sunday school teachers, and cooking for the elders and pastors. When it comes to teaching in the church, they are not allowed to use the pulpit to teach, and in most cases they are not allowed to preach. Therefore, when God calls women into ordained ministry, they are not ordained, based on what the constitution says: "it is the policy of ECWA not to licence or ordain women in conformity with 1 Timothy 2:11-12."[4] Although it is stated in the *Minister's Handbook* that "ECWA recognizes that God sets apart by His gracious will, individuals within the church for duties as evangelists, pastors, teachers, elders, administrators, etc. In recognition of His divine will, the church shall publicly set apart officers, for duties by dedicating, licencing and ordination exercise,"[5] women are subjugated since they are denied the privilege of serving God and God's people in an ordained capacity. If ECWA were to honour faithfully the statement delineated above, then women ought to be ordained as well, since the church recognizes that it is God who sets apart individuals for service.

One of the reasons used to justify the exclusion of women from ordained ministry is culture. Culture is the "customary beliefs and values that ethnic, religious, and social groups transmit fairly unchanged from generation to generation."[6] As such, culture has the power to shape our everyday behaviours, influencing the important decisions we make in life. That is why Anyalebechi postulates that the cultures of many societies are characterized by subjugating women to men and undermining their worth.[7] Bwire argues that African traditional culture has been a common obstacle and the cause of gender inequity.[8] The perpetuation of inequalities in society begins early in life, in the way children are socialized. Girls are trained to be good housewives, respectful, dependent on men in terms of protection, leadership, and financial support. Meanwhile, boys are trained to be strong, leaders, decision makers, superior to girls, and independent. Anyalebechi argues that in Nigeria, women are

---

4. ECWA Constitution and by-laws, 2019:43.

5. ECWA Minister's Handbook, 31.

6. Guiso, Sapienza, and Zingales, 2006:23.

7. Linda Anyalebechi, "The Issue of Gender Inequality in Nigeria," *Journal of Policy and Development Studies* 10: 2 (May 2016), 63–71.

8. John Bwire, "Practicing Biblical Equity," in *The Quest for Gender Equity in Leadership*, ed. Keumju Jewel Hyun and Diphus C. Chemorion (Eugene: Wipf & Stock, 2016), 182.

discriminated against in politics, churches, offices, and even families.[9] Women are considered as lesser human beings compared to men. That is why raising the issue of gender equality, and particularly including women in ordained ministry, is seen as trying to strip men of their power.

These cultures have found their way into the church, as is evident in the existing attitudes toward women and men in spite of Jesus' teaching in Matthew 15:6: "For the sake of your tradition, you make void the word of God." The Bible has often been sacrificed at the altar of culture.[10] This has contributed to my raising questions about the exclusion of women in leadership roles in my church through the use of 1 Timothy 2:12. Mbugua correctly notes that "women are allowed to take the same courses with men in Bible colleges, seminaries, and most of their teachers are women, but they are not ordained at the end. Most churches have used and twisted Biblical doctrines against women inclusion as ordained ministers."[11] The churches continue to misapply generic terms to promote male supremacy over female, who are already experiencing unfair treatment in various spheres of their lives.[12]

Apart from culture, patriarchal interpretations of the Bible are also used to exclude women from ordained ministry. This is a male-centred worldview which values the man as superior and sees the woman as inferior. It has to do with patriarchal dominance in interpreting the Bible, which supports male dominance and superiority in leadership. Patriarchy is found in most cultures, even in theology, where for a long time the dominant interpretations of the Bible have been patriarchal and Western-oriented As Justin Ukpong rightly says, there is a need for Africans to have their mode of interpretation based on our context and realities as the communities receiving the text rather than on those who produce it.[13] A lack of such interpretations has led to gender injustice in the Anglican Church of Nigeria and ECWA, among other churches where women are marginalized in leadership. Throughout history, women have been denied leadership roles based on certain interpretations of

---

9. Anyalebechi, "The Issue of Gender Inequality," 64.

10. Judy Mbugua, E. Leevathi Manasse, Nora Matilda Mendez de Mora and Russell Palsrok, "How Culture Affects the Roles of Women and Men in Ministry," in *Empowering Women and Men to Use Their Gifts Together in Advancing the Gospel*, ed. Alvera Mickelsen (Thailand: Lausanne Occasional Paper No. 53, 2004), 69.

11. Ibid.

12. Oduyoye and Kanyoro, *The Will to Arise*, 140.

13. Mary Getui, Tinyiko Maluleke and Justin Ukpong, eds., *Interpreting the New Testament in Africa* (Nairobi: Acton Publishers, 2001), 11.

the teachings of St Paul. Even today, some churches continue to suggest that the Bible prohibits women from leadership and preaching roles, often based on a certain interpretation of 1 Timothy 2:11-15.[14]

In the words of Dube, to read the Bible as a Motswana African woman is to read a Western book.[15] This is in reference to the missionaries who brought the gospel with their Western culture, which contributes to women being marginalized in the church. In Nigerian churches, the traditional teachings of missionaries propagated the notion that women's important role was in the domestic and not the public domain.[16] Bwire argues that African Christian leaders can turn to the Bible to help bolster women's place in the church, but men, who are the majority in leadership, still choose to interpret the biblical text in a way that demeans women.[17] Some women are satisfied with and have accepted male leadership roles in the church. Others (women and men, including me) do not accept the status quo and are thus committed to challenging the oppression and marginalization of women in church leadership. Oduyoye rightly observes that throughout Africa, the Bible has been and continues to be absolutized: it is one of the oracles we consult for instant solutions and responses.[18] Nigeria has a budding association of Nigerian biblicists. For Oduyoye, biblicists are people who hold the position that whatever is in the Bible is true. They have reservations about any critical interpretation of the Bible which they term "liberal." For biblicists, literal interpretations are the ideal.

Njoroge explains that women do not address philosophical or abstract ideas but rather "are dealing with today's life-threatening/destroying and life-giving/affirming issues. Doing theology means wrestling with God's Word as we confront the powers and principalities of this world."[19]

---

14. Mimi Haddad, "The Biblical Basis for Women's Gospel Service," in *Empowering Women and Men to Use Their Gifts Together in Advancing the Gospel,* ed. Alvera Mickelsen (Thailand: Lausanne Occasional Paper No. 53, 2004), 27.

15. Musa W. Dube, "Towards a Post-colonial Feminist Interpretation of the Bible," *Journal Semeia* 98 (1997), 11.

16. N.J. Njoroge, *Kiama Kia Ngo: An African Christian Feminist Ethic of Resistance and Transformation* (Ghana: LTSS, 2000), 58; Philomena Njeri Mwaura, "Gender Equity and Empowerment in African Public Theology: The Case of the Circle of Concerned African Women Theologians," July 2015, https://www.eldis.org/document/A101383.

17. Bwire, "Practicing Biblical Equity," 185.

18. Mercy Amba Oduyoye, *Daughters of Anowa: African Women and Patriarchy* (Maryknoll: Orbis, 1995), 174.

19. N.J. Njoroge, "The Missing Voice: African Women Doing Theology," *Journal of Theology for*

But for most ECWA theologians, doing theology is more about abstract and philosophical ideas which probably do not affect the realities of what people are going through in the church. Isabel Apawo Phiri observes the various challenges that African women theologians are facing, such as the challenge of their identity, empowering women to study theology and teach in theological institutions, and collaborating with male African theologians.[20] These challenges also apply to women's ordination in Nigeria. In fact, several colleagues at St. Paul's University have told me they have observed that so far, only men are coming from Nigeria to further their studies in theology. They wonder whether no women in Nigeria can also come to further their theological studies in Kenya or elsewhere. Empowering women in ECWA to study theology seems to be a waste of resources, since after the training she will not be ordained, or she may end up getting married to a man from a different denomination. For these reasons, few male theologians will support women's inclusion in the church. Most male theologians have probably been trained in the patriarchal interpretation of the Bible and have neglected other ways of reading and interpreting the Bible.

1 Timothy 2:12 and the Ordination of Women in ECWA

The letter of 1 Timothy has received scholarly attention as one of the pastoral letters of Paul, although there is much dispute about the authorship of this letter. One issue is the writing style, which is not found in other Pauline letters. The tone, vocabulary, style, theology, and apparent circumstances of the first letter to Timothy are quite different from other letters Paul wrote in the 50s and 60s CE.[21] Thus, many scholars have posited that the letter was not written by Paul, but by an admirer of his who wanted to bring Paul's voice and authority to a later set of crises. Though it cannot be dated with any certainty, there is some agreement that the letter was written around the end of the first century.[22] Other scholars consider the vocabulary, which differs from other Pauline letters. The historical situation of the pastoral

---

Southern Africa 99 (1997), 77–83.

20. Phiri Isabel Apawo, "Major Challenges for African Women Theologians in Theological Education (1989–2008)," *International Review of Mission* 98: 1 (2009), DOI: 10.1111/j.1758-6631.2009.00009.

21. Paul Trebilco, *The Early Christians in Ephesus from Paul to Ignatius* (Tubingen: Mohr Siebeck, 2004), 197–99.

22. Mona Tokarek La Fosse, "Women's Roles in the Letters to Timothy and Titus," in *Women in the Bible,* ed. Robert B. Kruschwitz (Waco: The Center for Christian Ethics at Baylor University, 2013), 30.

letters does not reflect the situation of Paul's life as recorded in Acts and in the genuine letters of Paul. But Black et al. argue that Paul was the author based on theological statements concerning humanity and salvation as well as the creativity Paul displays in being receptive to the thought of other makers of Christian theology.[23] Mbamalu further argues that Paul was more of age when writing the pastoral epistles than when writing other letters. In fact, the pastoral letters were believed to be his last.[24]

At the time the apostle Paul wrote this letter to Timothy, the church in Ephesus was struggling under the increased attacks of false teachers from within. Ephesus is believed to have been the centre of pagan worship; it presented a great challenge for the Christian mission.[25] The message of the letter is to provide instructions and sound teaching for the organization and administration of the church and to combat heresies that threatened to destroy the church (1 Tim. 4:1–6:2). In addition, 1 Timothy 3:14-15 gives a clear indication of the purpose. The phrase "I do not permit a woman to teach or to have authority over a man" also appears (1 Tim. 2:12 RSV). Does that mean that a woman can never teach or take on leadership responsibility over men or in a local church? What was Paul trying to address in this context? How should modern readers read and understand what Paul is saying from its historical context? How did Timothy, the recipient of the letter, understand it? And how should we in ECWA understand this passage? This essay will also consider other passages of Paul's letters to comprehend what Paul meant by inclusion or exclusion of women in ministry.

Elna Mouton observes that the background and Paul's whole experience must be kept in mind if we are to interpret this letter fairly,[26] such as passages of his letters where he knew of women prophesying (Acts 21:8ff) and his recommendations about women (Acts 18:1-3; Rom. 16:3ff; 1 Cor. 16:19, among others). Considering the background to the text, Keener argues that some women in Antiquity had the opportunity to learn and become leaders;

23. Robert Black and Ronald McClung, *1 & 2 Timothy, Titus, and Philemon: A Commentary for Bible Students* (Indianapolis: Wesleyan House, 2004), 114.

24. Abiola I. Mbamalu, "'The Woman Was Deceived and Became a Sinner': A Literary-Theological Investigation of 1 Timothy 2:11-15," HTS Teologiese Studies/Theological Studies 70: 3 (2014), 3–4, http://dx.doi.org/10.4102/hts.v70i3.2062.

25. Andreas Köstenberger, "1 and 2 Timothy, Titus," in *Expositor's Bible Commentary: Ephesians – Philemon*, ed. Tremper Longman III and David E. Garland (Grand Rapids: Zondervan, 2006), 490.

26. Elna Mouton, "Teaching a Pastoral 'Text of Terror' in Africa Today? I Timothy 2:8-15 as a Context-specific Appropriation of the Creation Story," (2011), 2–3,

only a tiny proportion of respected sages (such as Aspasia, Sosipatra, and Hypatia) were women who could also teach men.[27] What Paul is addressing in this passage, according to Keener, was the false teachers targeting women, who were considered vulnerable to these false teachings and might in turn teach others. Most of the women during the Greco-Roman period were probably not trained in scripture.[28] Mouton observes that the context Paul was addressing has to do with conduct of Christians in the general assembly, in which prayers are to be made for rulers (2:1-4), where conflict may mar their prayers (2:8); Paul's admonition is not for life generally, but in the gathering of God's people and the specific situation of the assembly.[29]

Most scholars are divided on whether the verb ἐπιτρέπω ("permit" or "allow") is temporal or universal in nature. This verb – which can also mean to turn to, to give up to, to commit to one's care, to entrust to, to trust to, to give way to, to suffer, to permit, to refer to, to concede, to agree to, or even to command – is a present active indicative. The indicative carries less universal force than an imperative, which is more of a command.[30] In classical times, the verb could also mean to play the part of a mediator.[31] Black et al. argue that "if Paul means for the prohibition of women from teaching to be a divine imperative, it is strange that he does not use an imperative form of the verb."[32] Furthermore, Grenz and Kjesbo observed that if Paul had used an imperative, which would be rendered as "Do not allow a woman to teach," it would be easier to understand his prohibition as being permanent.[33] Instead, the present indicative says that "Paul is not voicing a timeless command, but a temporary directive applicable to a specific situation: 'I am not presently allowing.'"[34] Samuel Ngewa agrees with Grenz and Kjesbo that the phrase "I do not permit" indicates that Paul is here giving his own opinion rather than making an authoritative statement.[35] Paul was responding to the false teaching that was going on in the church and

---

27. Craig S. Keener, *The IVP Bible Background Commentary*, 2nd ed. (Westmont: IVP Academic, 2014), 605.

28. Ibid., 606.

29. Mouton, "Teaching a Pastoral 'Text of Terror' in Africa Today," 3–4.

30. Horst Balz & Gerhard Schneider, 1991:43.

31. Richard Clark and Catherine Clark, *I Suffer Not a Woman: Rethinking 1 Timothy 2:11-15 in Light of Ancient Evidence* (Grand Rapids: Baker Academic, 1992), 83.

32. Black and McClung, *1 & 2 Timothy, Titus, and Philemon*, 66.

33. Stanley J. Grenz and Denise Muir Kjesbo, *Women in the Church: A Biblical Theology of Women in Ministry* (Downers Grove: InterVarsity, 1995), 130.

34. Ibid.

35. Samuel M. Ngewa, *1 & 2 Timothy and Titus* (Grand Rapids: Zondervan, 2009), 52.

the fact that women were being used to teach the false doctrine.

Some scholars do not see the fact of the present indicative as undoubtedly showing that the prevention is temporary. In Marshall's words, "nothing can be determined from the aspect or from the verb itself as to the length of time that the injunction would be in effect."[36] Mounce agrees with Marshall, saying that "while the use of the present tense does not require that a statement be true in the future, neither is there anything in the tense that requires it to be true only in the present but not later."[37] The verse begins with διδάσκειν, meaning "to teach," which expresses the content of teaching, whether the word of God or false doctrines which opponents promulgated (1 Tim. 1:3, 7; 4:1; 6:3). This Greek word, as used in 1 Timothy, shows that somehow women are involved in teaching false doctrine. So if one concludes that the word διδάσκειν prohibits women from teaching, then such an interpreter will find difficulty with other pastoral passages, such as Titus 2:3, 2 Timothy 2:2, and 2 Timothy 1:5.[38] George Knight observes that Paul uses functional language, "to teach," rather than office language, "Bishop," to express the prohibition – not on ministerial work but on the context in which women are used to promote false teaching in the church.[39]

Cynthia Long Westfall argues that the word αὐθεντεῖν has been debated, with some scholars assuming that the word connotes "being a Pastor," whose primary justification is to exclude women from ministry.[40] But Long Westfall argues that none of the usages of the word refer to any kind of pastoral care or church official. Linda Belleville shows how αὐθεντεῖν has been translated from "murderer, in the wisdom of Solomon 12:6," to "original or authentic in 3 Maccabees 2:28-29" and "to have [or exercise] authority over."[41] If Paul wanted to speak of exercise of authority, he could have chosen from a number of words that convey that idea. But Paul probably used αὐθεντεῖν because it carried a

36. I. Howard Marshall and Philip H. Towner, *A Critical and Exegetical Commentary on the Pastoral Epistles* (Edinburgh: T&T Clark, 1999), 454.

37. William D. Mounce, *Word Biblical Commentary 46: Pastoral Epistles,* ed. Bruce M. Metzger (Nashville: Thomas Nelson, 2000), 122–23.

38. Clark and Clark, *I Suffer Not a Woman,* 81–82.

39. George Knight, *The Pastoral Epistles* (Grand Rapids: Eerdmans, 1992), 141.

40. Cynthia Long Westfall, *Paul and Gender: Reclaiming the Apostle's Vision for Men and Women in Christ* (Grand Rapids: Baker Academic, 2016), 291.

41. Linda L. Belleville, "Teaching and Usurping Authority: I Timothy 2:11-15," in *Discovering Biblical Equality: Complementarity without Hierarchy,* ed. Ronald W. Pierce and Rebecca Merrill Groothuis (Downers Grove: IVP Academic, 2005), 211.

nuance (other than a rule or having authority) that was particularly suited to the situation in Ephesus. Paul seems to be concerned with women who are teaching false doctrine rather than exercising general authority over men, which is different from the context of 1 Timothy 2:12.[42]

It should be observed that if Paul had the ordinary exercise of ecclesiastical leadership and authority in mind, he had at his disposal a number of words that could have served this sense, notably proḯstēmi. Paul's use of the word in reference to church leaders (1 Tim. 3:4, 5, 12; 5:17; 1 Thess. 5:12; Rom. 12:8) has the senses of "manage, conduct, rule, direct, be concerned about"; it connotes the "normal" and "expected" type of leadership that should be exhibited by those selected to lead.[43] The fact that a highly unusual and ambiguous word is chosen in 1 Timothy 2:12 would fit an unusual set of circumstances in the context to which the text is addressed. As has been argued above, these circumstances, as indicated in the letter itself, involve women who are being deceived by false teachers and as such are not suitable for the exercise of teaching or ruling authority in Ephesus.

Gender Justice in ECWA

The quest for equity in leadership is a fight for justice which must go on until victory is achieved.[44] Reading and interpreting 1 Timothy 2:12 in line with gender justice in ECWA, an interpreter needs to bear in mind the context in which the letter was written. An interpreter needs to understand that Paul wanted women to learn so they could teach. If Paul prohibits women from teaching because they are not learned, his demand that they learn constitutes a long-range solution to the problem. Women who are not learned in the scriptures could not be trusted to pass on its teachings accurately, but once they had learned, this would not be an issue; they could join the ranks of women in the ministry together with men, which Keener agrees was the context of 1 Timothy 2:12.[45] Modupe Owanikin agrees with Keener that "it is significant to note that Paul's stance on women's role in the church is not essentially antifeminist but rather arises from his recognition of the women

---

42. Thomas Geer, "Admonition to Women in 1 Timothy 2:8-15," in *Essays on Women in Earliest Christianity,* ed. Carroll D. Osburn (Joplin: College Press, 1993), 294.

43. Balz & Gerhard, 1990.

44. Diphus C. Chemorion and Hyun Keumju Jewel, "Conclusion," in *The Quest for Gender Equity in Leadership,* ed. Keumju Jewel Hyun and Diphus C. Chemorion (Eugene: Wipf & Stock, 2016), 211.

45. Keener, *The IVP Bible Background Commentary,* 112.

church leaders of his time."[46] Such women include Priscilla and Aquila, Lydia, Junia, and Phoebe – active missionaries and leaders in the early church who travelled with Paul to spread the gospel and who used their properties to house the churches. That is why Paul has to commend them and also rec- ognize their leadership roles in the churches.

Since ECWA upholds the Bible as the inspired word of God, then right interpretation should be explored to be able to bring out the meaning of 1 Timothy 2:12, which the church is using to exclude women from ordination. Reading 1 Timothy from its context of Paul's writing will yield a better interpretation instead of taking it literally, at face value. ECWA needs to understand that Paul's instruction is not to be seen as universal, but rather arising from the context the church in Ephesus is facing. In fact, Paul acknowledged that women have prophetic gifts and are involved in the ministry of the church (Rom. 16:1-15; 1 Cor. 11:5; Phil. 4:2-3). In addition, he challenged the contemporary view on women by noting that in Christ there is neither male nor female (Gal. 3:28); thus, Paul neutralized gender and offers a gender-inclusive promise of redemption through Christ Jesus. Oduyoye rightly observes that "whatever is keeping subordination of women alive in the church cannot be the Spirit of God. The church is intended to be the ecclesia of all people, women and men, across all social barriers."[47]

There are many women in ECWA seminaries who are preparing men and women in the study of theology and those who have already been trained. Both men and women need to be empowered and liberated to be able to see one another as co-workers in God's kingdom. As Oduyoye notes, African churches need to empower women not only to speak for themselves but also to include right and critical interpretations of biblical text, its theology, and how it should be applied to our context.[48] Only then will the church become a home to both men and women. Oduyoye furthers observe that

> liberation must be viewed as men and women walking together on the journey home, with the church as the umbrella of faith, hope, and love. The church must shed its image as a male organization with a female clientele whom it placates with vain promises, half-truths, and the prospect of redemption at the end of time.

---

46. Modupe R. Owanikin, "The Priesthood of Church Women in the Nigerian Context," in Oduyoye and Kanyoro, *The Will to Arise*, 215.

47. Oduyoye, *Daughters of Anowa*, 182.

48. Ibid., 181.

Both men and women need liberation from androcentric cultural modes of interpretation and need to move to a holistic and inclusive mode of interpretation. Men need to see women not as a threat but as those who are called by God and created in the image and likeness of God. Men need to be aware of how the same patriarchal system oppresses them as men and so take adequate measures to liberate themselves.[49] ECWA theologians need to embrace other ways of reading and interpreting the Bible: reading through the lens of women is the key to fighting gender injustice in the church. Allowing women to speak for themselves and undertaking a critical interpretation of scripture, such as a postcolonial feminist reading of the Bible, will yield a better understanding of scripture.

Conclusion

This essay has noted that with regard to the ordination of women in ECWA, gender justice has been neglected due to cultural reasons and a patriarchal interpretation of 1 Timothy 2:12. Having been exposed to other ways of interpreting the Bible, such as reading and interpreting through the lens of women, I am convinced that 1 Timothy 2:12 is not intended to prohibit women from being ordained. Rather, it is a context-specific injunction directed to women, who were not well trained and were thus spreading false teaching, to learn first before teaching others. I am also challenging patriarchal and gender-biased interpretations of the Bible, which are used to oppress the calling of women to ordained ministry. Using other ways of interpreting the Bible, especially a postcolonial feminist reading, will yield a better understanding and interpretation of the Bible.

Interpretations of scripture passages which do not consider the biblical context carefully will often lead to wrong theology, which will be used to oppress women. A clear understanding of 1 Timothy 2:12 from its historical context has clearly shown that Paul was not giving an imperative command. In other letters, Paul commended women leaders of the churches. In interpreting this passage, an interpreter needs to consider the historical situation, where Paul seems to be addressing how women are being used to teach false doctrine. If Paul, in other letters, acknowledges women as leaders of churches, then ECWA should consider ordaining women who are teachers in their seminaries and have completed theological training for ministry.

---

49. Teresa Okure, "Invitation to African Women's Hermeneutical Concerns," in Getui, Maluleke and Ukpong, *Interpreting the New Testament in Africa,* 53.

8

Female Clergy in Rwanda as Agents of Changing Patriarchal Understanding in the Pilgrimage of Justice and Peace

Rev. Francoise Niyonsaba

Abstract

This essay reflects on the situation of female clergy in the context of Rwanda. It is a contribution to gender justice as we focus on "The Africa We Pray for on a Pilgrimage of Justice and Peace." It uses feminist theory to argue that female and male have equal rights in church ministry because God created humans in God's image and gave them the authority to rule over the earth. In addition, the church should follow the example of Jesus, who did not segregate anyone. The mission of the church should be inclusive in all areas: in evangelism, in the administration of the sacraments, and in church leadership. Women should be allowed to be free and active participants in church ministry.

Introduction

The Jewish and Christian religions grew out of a patriarchal society – a world where men dominated in all areas of life, including politics, religion, the economy, and at home. Everyone assumed it was true that women and slaves, and even children to some extent, were inferior to men and were simply their possessions. Many societies in the world still operate on the assumption of male superiority.[1] This essay intends to respond to gender injustice in the church. It examines Jesus' view of women as a transformative action versus the church's practices today. It also studies women in church leadership and female clergy as agents of change in churches of Africa.

This study will use feminist theory to analyze female clergy's experience in church ministry. Even given their strong numbers, women's performance has been strictly limited by the patriarchal structures and teachings of the church. Hosken said that feminist theories are the most significant theories used for analyzing the status of women and men in society while trying to bring a

---

1. Norwegian Church Aid, *Created in God's Image: A Gender Transformation Toolkit for Women and Men in Churches,* "Tool 3: Exploring How the Bible Talks about Women and Men," n.d., https://www.kirkensnodhjelp.no/contentassets/c2cd7731ab1b4727897258c5d49246c8/nca-createdingodsimage-tool03-jun2015-open2.pdf.

change to women's subordination, which is caused and reinforced by gender inequalities in patriarchal societies.[2] Feminist theories will help to show that all forms of oppressive language used to describe the church – including texts that describe institutions which oppress and marginalize women and exclude them from all essential processes of representation and self-definition – will be critically examined by feminist theology. Watson observed that feminist theologians have found that churches which understood themselves as being churches of the word have been a place where women suffer institutional injustice, where women are told of their supposed insignificance.[3] Therefore, African women theologians have argued that the starting point for African women's engagement with the church and culture are women's experiences.[4] That is why this essay has used African feminist theories to investigate the importance of women clergy in the church in Rwanda.

Jesus' View of Women as Transformative Action

The revolutionary foundation Jesus established for women's equality is revealed in the gospel narratives. This equality was so contrary to Jewish law and the customs of the time that it shocked Jesus' contemporaries. Pope John Paul II said, "When it comes to setting women free from every kind of exploitation and domination, the Gospel contains an ever-relevant message which goes back to the attitude of Jesus Christ himself."[5] The challenge here is that many Christians ignore the liberating strands in our scriptures. They tend to focus on the patriarchal ideas which support their own social or cultural views about women's inferiority. This raises questions about the way our cultural and social prejudices affect how we read the scriptures.[6] Also, church dogma is being used to strengthen unjust systems instead of challenging them and making them instruments of healing, restoration, and redemption.[7] For this

2. F.P. Hosken, *Genital and Sexual Mutilation of Females,* 2nd ed. (Lexington: Women's International Network News, 1979).

3. Natalie K. Watson, *Introducing Feminist Ecclesiology* (Sheffield: Sheffield Academic Press, 2002), 2–3.

4. Isabel Apawo Phiri and Sarojini Nadar, eds, *African Women, Religion, and Health: Essays in Honour of Mercy Amba Ewudziwa Oduyoye* (Maryknoll: Orbis, 2006).

5. Pope John Paul II, "Letter to Women," 29 June 1995, http://www.vatican.va/content/john-paul-ii/en/letters/1995/documents/hf_jp-ii_let_29061995_women.html.

6. Michael Hilton and Gordon Marshall, *The Gospel and Rabbinic Judaism: A Study Guide* (London: SCM Press, 1988), 128.

7. Teresa Stanton Collette, "Independence or Interdependence? A Christian Response to Liberal Feminists," in *Christian Perspectives in Legal Thought 178,* ed. Michael W. McConnell, Robert F. Cochran, Jr. and Angela C. Carmella (New Haven: Yale University Press, 2001).

reason, the church would be the inclusive place where all people share equal rights and abundant life.

Furthermore, Jesus' positive view of women is consistently evident in all four gospels. He treated women as equals and definitely not as sex objects or as personal or legal possessions. Jesus considered women worthy of being part of his circle. He conferred equal dignity and personhood on women in a culture and time when they were not considered worthy.[8] He presented educational opportunities to women, referring to this as "the better part," and commissioned them as credible witnesses at a time when women were not legally recognized as legitimate witnesses in a court or on any matter. He trusted women with the good news of his resurrection, and a woman offered testimony of his identity to an entire village[9] – this crossed cultural boundaries, the taboo line for Jews, in transforming her life. In one simple encounter with a Samaritan woman, Jesus' respect for her, regardless of her gender, religion, or marital status, meant that his message transformed people's lives.

The Pilgrimage of Justice and Peace cannot succeed or reach its goal unless the church leaves behind prejudice and cultural ties that segregate human beings. Martin Luther King, Jr said, "We've learned to fly the air as birds, we've learned to swim the seas as fish. But yet we haven't learned to walk the earth as brothers and sisters."[10]

Surprisingly, in many churches, women are voiceless and considered unworthy to participate in church activities. Mombo and Joziasse argue that "even the great number of church members are women but for some reasons the status of women in the pews and men in leadership roles is taken for granted."[11] In preaching and in the liturgy, women are largely excluded,

---

8. Carolyn Custis James, Lost Women of the Bible: *The Women We Thought We Knew* (Grand Rapids: Zondervan, 2005), 189.

9. Lynne Marie Kohm, "A Christian Perspective on Gender Equality," *Duke Journal of Gender Law & Policy* 15: 339 (2008), 339–63, https://core.ac.uk/download/pdf/62547986.pdf.

10. PBS, "When MLK Jr. Lamented 'We Have Not Learned the Simple Art of Living Together," 18 January 2016,

https://www.pbs.org/newshour/show/when-mlk-jr-lamented-we-have-not-learned-the-simple-art-of-living-together.

11. Esther Mombo and Heleen Joziasse, *If You Have No Voice, Just Sing! Narratives of Women's Lives and Theological Education at St. Paul's University* (Limuru: Zapf Chancery, 2011), 3.

and their issues do not form part of the major agenda in the church.[12] The Presbyterian Church of Rwanda is the church that has a great number of women pastors and theologians. Unfortunately, other churches still exclude women from church mission. Some are ordaining a few women, but others are not, because of sociocultural norms that undermine women and because of poor interpretations of scripture. The Pilgrimage of Justice and Peace has a long way to go to achieve gender justice in the church, but it is possible.

Women in Church Leadership

The ordination of women to ministerial or priestly offices is an increasingly common practice among some major religious groups today. But it remains a controversial issue in certain Christian denominations, where ordination has for almost 2,000 years been limited to men.[13] The laws and traditions against the ordination of women are often smokescreens. Some women contend that the real problem is male attitudes developed over 20 centuries. Female rabbinical candidates make a strong case for ordination on the basis that women had a higher position in early Jewish society than in any corresponding culture: "Women received revelation the same as men."[14] Jan Kaufman, a senior professor at Hebrew Union College, the Reform seminary in New York, said, "I have no problem invoking God of Sara, Rachel and Rebekah, just as I would say God of Abraham, Isaac and Moses."[15] This is to witness that women are as gifted by God to perform religious activities as men are.

Furthermore, in some cases, women have been permitted to be ordained but not to hold higher positions in the church. While laws prohibit sex discrimination in employment, exceptions are often made for clergy.16 For example, Rwanda has signed the Convention on the Elimination of All Forms of Discrimination against Women. The convention says that parties shall take all appropriate measures to eliminate discrimination against women in the political and public life of the country and, in particular, shall ensure

---

12. Esther Mombo and Heleen Joziasse, "From the Pew to the Pulpit: Engendering the Pulpit through Teaching 'African Women's Theologies,'" in *Men in the Pulpit, Women in the Pew: Addressing Gender Inequality in Africa*, ed. Jurgens Hendriks, Elna Mouton, Len Hansen and Elisabet Le Roux (Stellenbosch: African Sun Press, 2012), 193.

13. BBC, *"Women Bishops Vote: Church of England 'Resembles Sect,'" 22 November 2012*, https://www.bbc.com/news/uk-politics-20443718.

14. Ibid.

15. George Vescey, "Women's Ordination Grows as a Major Religious Issue, *New York Times,* 12 November 1978), 26.

16. Ibid.

that women are on equal terms with men, including the rights to vote in all elections and public referenda and to be eligible for election to all publicly elected bodies.17 Also, the Constitution of the Republic of Rwanda commits the state to ensure equal rights between Rwandans and between men and women without prejudice to the principles of gender equality and complementarity in national development.18 This is practical because, for example, Rwanda has one of the highest representations of women in Parliament in the world. If women can hold higher positions in the government and they perform well, why not in the church?

Here one can ask why the participation of women in church leadership is limited even in those traditions that accept the ordination of women, when in most churches they constitute a larger part of church membership. It is clear that one reason lies in the way biblical texts on gender have been used – or misused. The Bible was produced by many authors and written in various diverse sociocultural settings over many centuries. That is why the church needs to understand the tension between the meaning of the word in our contemporary context and the historical context of the Bible texts.[19] But again, a good solution can be for the church to learn from the Rwandan government on how it is dealing with gender justice. Within the church, we might celebrate life together while eliminating any form of discrimination against women, where everyone in the church sees their neighbour as themselves.

Spiritually speaking, authority is not grounded in maleness. Both women and men were given the authority to rule over the earth. There is no biologically based inequality in creational authority, personal agency, or responsibilities.[20] The Old Testament teaches us that both men and women are created in the image of God (Gen. 1:26-27). According to Paul, all believers, men and women. conform to the image of God (Rom. 8:29). Despite the fact that gender traditionalists argue that the ministry of prophet included some functions that excluded women, both women and men were recognized as prophets and judges in ancient Israel; prime examples are Deborah and

---

17. Marie-anne Dushimimana, "Women Urged to Take up More Leadership Positions,"
The New Times, 20 May 2018, https://www.newtimes.co.rw/news/women-urged-take-more-leadership-positions.

18. Ibid.

19. Elisabeth Schüssler Fiorenza, *Bread Not Stone: The Challenge of Feminist Biblical Interpretation* (Boston: Beacon Press, 1984), 23.

20. Ronald W. Pierce & Rebecca Merrill Groothuis (2nd Ed), *Discovering Biblical Equality: Complementarity Without Hierarchy* (Downers Grove: InterVarsity Press, 2005), 87-95

Huldah (2 Kings 22:14-19; Chron. 34:23-27).[21] In addition, some passages in the New Testament tell of women who were called to ministries that involved teaching and leading assemblies of both men and women (e.g., Rom. 16:7, Acts 21:9).[22]

Susan Rackoczy notes that in the Bible, women were not only apostles and prophets, but also preachers, deacons, and evangelists; they even presided over the Eucharist.[23] This is to confirm that if God decreed that these positions are unsuitable for women because they are women, this example would not exist.[24] I am convinced that as equal heirs, men and women have equal rights and responsibilities, the same access to and right to represent God and to obey God's commands. Every believer has been given the priestly ministry of representing Christ to the church and the world and is directly accountable to God. Groothuis argues that in their dealing with human beings, God and Christ do not favour those of one gender above the other; as followers of Christ and children of God, we need to do the same.[25] The World Council of Churches' Pilgrimage of Justice and Peace can reach its transformative actions when the global church understands that women and men have equal rights in the church's ministry and equal shares in God's kingdom. All churches should allow women to be eligible for the higher positions in church leadership.

Referring to the African context, in African Traditional Religion, women have had the same rights in leadership. Mbiti states that "in many areas there were [and still are] women priests (Priestesses). Almost everywhere in Africa, those who are so important in traditional medical practice are nearly always women, those who experience spirit possession are in most cases women."[26] Unfortunately, the statistics gathered in 2012 on gender representation in church offices in 25 Protestant Reformed churches in Africa show that the number of women who serve as pastors is 4 percent; in high positions, 95.3 percent are men and 0.7 percent are women.[27] This affirms that the majority

---

21. Ibid.

22. Harawa K. Chimwemwe, *The Bible, Gender Equality and Teaching Theology in Malawi* California: Mayfield Publishing 2012), 108.

23. Susan Rakoczy, *In Her Name: Women Doing Theology* (Pietermaritzburg: Cluster Publications, 2004), 202–207.

24. Ibid.

25. Ibid.

26. K. Appiah-Kubi, *Man Cures, God Heals* (New York: Friendship Press, 1981), 30–40.

27. Jurgens Hendriks, "Churches, Seminaries and Gender Statistics," in *Men in the Pulpit, Women in the Pew: Addressing Gender Inequality in Africa,* ed. Jurgens Hendriks, Elna Mouton,Len Hansen and Elisabet Le Roux (Stellenbosch: African Sun Press, 2012), 25–32, at 26–29.

of Reformed African churches do not recognize the role of women on an equal scale in religious leadership. Even though Christianity is a religion of liberation and inclusiveness, when it comes to church leadership, women are still excluded by many churches in Africa. The church should recognize that all human beings were created to complement each other and that they all have equal rights in the kingdom of God. The mother of African women theologians, Mercy Amba Oduyoye, at the Circle of Concerned African Women Theologians' 1989 conference in Accra, argued that African Christianity needs to do "two-winged theology." For her, a bird cannot fly with one wing; two are needed. The same is true of Christian practices: the intervention of both men and women is needed. This can be the theology through which both men and women can communicate with God.[28]

In the precolonial period, women in Rwanda played an important role in the country's governance through the institution of the Queen Mother.[29] Today, the promotion of gender equality, which is Sustainable Development Goal 5, spans various aspects that affects women's lives, from access to education, to accessing political leadership, to participating in the decision-making process, among other aspects.[30] Therefore, African women acted, they still act, and they are able to fit into any leadership position, including church leadership. The church should recognize the abilities and gifts of women and allow them to hold higher positions in church leadership.

Female Clergy as Agents of Change in the African Church

A key theological doctrine for Reformed and other Protestant churches is the priesthood of all believers. This doctrine is considered so important that some have called it a truth of scripture.[31] This doctrine restores true dignity and true integrity to all believers, since it teaches that all believers are priests and that as priests, they are to serve God, no matter what legitimate vocation they pursue. Thus, no vocation is more sacred than any other. Because Christ is Lord over all areas of life, and because Christ's word applies to all areas of life, nowhere does Christ's word even remotely suggest that the ministry is sacred while all other vocations are secular. Scripture knows no sacred–secular distinction. All of life belongs to God. All of life is sacred. All

28. J.N. Njoroge, "The Missing Voice: African Women Doing Theology," *Journal of Theology of Southern Africa* 99 (1997), 77–83.

29. Jeanne Izabiliza, "The Role of Women in Reconstruction: Experience of Rwanda" n.d., http://www.unesco.org/new/fileadmin/MULTIMEDIA/HQ/SHS/pdf/Role-Women-Rwanda.pdf.

30. Ibid.

31. David Hagopian, "Trading Places: The Priesthood of All Believers" (Grace Chapel: The Center for Reformed Theology and Apologetics, 1990).

believers are priests.[32] Therefore, God's ministry is very inclusive of both men and women. The ordination of women in Protestant churches has been carried out in the light of this theological doctrine of the priesthood of all believers.

Many years ago, the ordained ministry was preserved for males only, but in the 20th century, an increasing number of denominations began ordaining women.

The church sees the entrance of women into ordained ministry as one of the most significant transformations of the 20th century; it has changed both the institutional lives of the churches as well as the lives of those women who have been ordained. Female clergy themselves are in a key position to change the church, and their role differs from church to church. Women, especially those in elite positions, have the potential to influence social change that benefits women's interests.[33]

In general, women clergy have a broader view of church work and regard most areas of church work as more important than do male clergy. Clergywomen put more emphasis on promoting equality, justice, and the rights of minorities than do clergymen. Half of the women clergy regarded promoting equality as very important in church work, compared to only one quarter of clergymen.[34] Women also regard helping people, supervising and mentoring, pastoral counselling, family work, education, and musical activities as more important than do men. This means that women clergy place more emphasis than clergymen do on tasks that can be regarded as performance. At the same time, there was a clear difference between men and women regarding how much the function is emphasized. This means that women clergy try to strongly apply religion and use their position as clergy to tackle various social problems – problems related to human dignity and inequality – while many of the men think the church should concentrate mainly on function and less on performance. Women's approach to work can be seen as a typically liberal approach, while men have a more conservative

---

32. Art Lindsley, "The Priesthood of All Believers" (Tysons: Institute for Faith, Work & Economics, 2013), https://tifwe.org/wp-content/uploads/2013/10/The-Priesthood-of-All-Believers-Lindsley.pdf.

33. Norwegian Church Aid, *Created in God's Image: A Gender Transformation Toolkit for Women and Men in Churches*, "Tool 9: Women in Church Leadership: Co-option or Transformation?" n.d., https://www.kirkensnodhjelp.no/contentassets/c2cd7731ab1b4727897258c5d49246c8/nca-createdingodsimage-tool09-jun2015-open2.pdf.

34. Kati Niemela, "Female Clergy as Agents of Religious Change?" *Religions* 2: 3 (2011), 358–71, https://www.mdpi.com/2077-1444/2/3/358.

view of church work.[35] Women also play a great role in advocacy for justice, which can bring many changes. Let us explore Numbers 27:1-8 and see how women can bring changes.

The story of Zelophehad's five daughters captures the challenges that women faced and what they had to do to affirm their rights with dignity. Numbers 26 describes a census taken of all males over the age of 20. As part of the list of the various clans, we read that Zelophehad had no sons, only daughters. As the census was concluded, God instructs Moses, "Among these shall the land be apportioned as shares." "Among these" refers to the males listed in the census. Hereafter, we can conclude that Zelophehad's daughters were not counted in the census and also were not to receive any land as inheritance. We might expect that women, heirs to Egyptian slavery and then put under law that frequently favours men, might react by keeping silent, by accepting as natural the rule decreed for them to follow. We might expect women in those days to stay close to their tents, remain out of sight, and not go far from their families. So how and why did Zelophehad's daughters write a new chapter in history? First, they dared to go out from their living place, from their social space, from the destiny imposed on them, from their cultural norms.

Moreover, the Israelite camp is formed of tribes, each of whom has a determined place, with the tabernacle in the middle. In the centre stand the main authority figures, all of them men: Moses, the priest Eleazar, and the tribal chief. Imposing as this structure may have been, the five sisters decided to claim their rights. Together, they go out of their tents, without being called by anyone, to the place where only the high-ranking men congregate, to the place where the tablets from Sinai rest in the Ark, to the place of holiness and authority, to a place where women did not have authority. The men must have been astonished when they saw such a surprising, exceptional situation. But this is not all that the five sisters do. They also speak with determination: "Our father died in the wilderness; he was not among the company of those who gathered together against the LORD in the company of Korah, but died for his own sin; and he had no sons. Why should the name of our father be taken away from his clan because he had no son? Give to us a possession among our father's brothers" (Num. 27:3-4).

These women knew their law and their history. They used the fact that their father was not involved in Korah's rebellion as evidence to support his and their claim to the land. They knew that the stability of the family name depends on inheritance of the land, and they realize that the current law was

---

35. Ibid.

not adequate, for it did not take into account the unusual circumstances of a man without sons. They possessed the insight to recognize this omission in God's law. But because they considered God's law to be just, or to aim to be just, they showed no hesitation in pointing out the unfair nature of the present situation with complete confidence and in supporting their claim with convincing arguments. A key to the sisters' success is their full awareness of God's laws and the people's history and story. They insisted on change by engaging Israelite traditions effectively, something the rabbinic sages recognized when they described the women.[36] The achievement of Zelophehad's daughters was an innovation in women's rights regarding the inheritance of land, from those days up to today. Finally, what these women did brought about strong changes because they were claiming their rights. Other women in Israel got the opportunity to inherit the land, and even today women have that right.

Therefore, the voice of women clergy plays a great role in advocating for peace and justice. In this pilgrimage of justice and peace, in order to transform people's lives, the church should hear and understand the voice of women. As shown above, women clergy put more emphasis on promoting equality, justice, and the rights of the minorities, because women can more easily approach people than men can when it comes to transformative actions. For example, in the Presbyterian Church of Rwanda, some women occupy higher positions, such as vice president and legal representative, as well as serving as presidents of presbyteries. These women are able to advocate for the rights of other women, and thus they help others to get a theological education. That is why there are many women theologians and pastors. They also mobilize women to be self-supporting rather than waiting for men to provide everything. Today, women are able to support their families. This leads to the development of the church and the country in general.

African women have always been active in agriculture, trade, and other economic pursuits, but most of them were in the informal labour force. African women were guardians of their children's welfare and have clear responsibilities to provide for them materially. They were the household managers, providing food, water, health, and education; there was widespread gender education.[37] Today, African

---

36. Silvina Chemen, "The Daughters of Zelophehad: Power and Uniqueness," in Tamara Cohn Eskenazi and Andrea L. Weiss, *The Torah: A Women's Commentary* (New York: URJ Press and Women of Reform Judaism, 2008), https://www.myjewishlearning.com/article/the-daughters-of-zelophehad-power-and-uniqueness.

37. Swasti Mitter and Sheila Rowbotham, *Women Encounter Technology: Changing Patterns of Employment in the Third World* (London: Routledge, 1995), 4.

women are active participants in peace building. For example, South Sudanese women have played a key role in resolving historical conflicts, which give them the experience and skills that are central in the current peace-building process. Women's activities in peace building support healing and reconciliation efforts.[38]

The sociocultural context in Rwanda before 1994 included polygamy. The majority of women did not enjoy the power of wealth because of their preoccupations as household managers. It was mostly men who worked to provide for the family. A woman was looked upon to carry out the family responsibilities.[39] After the 1994 genocide against the Tutsi, many families were headed by single parents; the number of orphans and groups headed by a minor increased. The government of Rwanda, wanting the wellbeing of all Rwandans, established the national policy for family promotion to empower women to increase the wellbeing of the Rwandan family.[40]

The way of thinking of women after the 1994 genocide improved; there was a major shift in gender roles because many widows who were the new heads of the family had to take up the roles of men. During the *Gacaca* courts, women took up the roles of being judges. Previously, such roles were reserved for the wise elders of the family, who were men. Women did well in ensuring that justice was served.[41] The empowerment of women by the Rwandan government was and is very helpful for the wellbeing of Rwandans and the development of Rwandan society. The Rwandan government works as much as it can to increase women's empowerment. This encourages women because they feel more powerful and more supported than before. Some men are proud of women's performance, too, and have decided to accompany them. Through gender balance, both men and women have equal rights, share in family properties, and work together for their development.

They celebrate life together. This demonstrates that if the church uses this approach of empowering women in transformative actions, great things can happen.

---

38. Nyathon James Hoth Mai, "The Role of Women in Peace Building in South Sudan," Policy Brief, The Sudd Institute, 1 December 2015, https://www.suddinstitute.org/publications/show/the-role-of-women-in-peace-building-in-south-sudan.

39. Government of Rwanda, National Policy for Family Promotion (2015), 4. https://www.ilo.org/dyn/natlex/docs/ELECTRONIC/92985/117299/F-1037879932/RWA-92985.pdf.

40. Ibid.

41. NURC, The Role Of Women In Reconciliation And Peace Building In Rwanda: Ten Years After Genocide 1994-2004: Contributions, Challenges and Way Forward, (2005), 32 https://repositories.lib.utexas.edu/bitstream/handle/2152/4786/3871.pdf;sequence=1.

After the 1994 genocide, there was a great need to mobilize and assist the population in reconstructing their lives as well as their communities and the country as a whole. Rwandese women played crucial roles in various leadership positions in mobilizing other women to live together and to find common solutions to their own problems and those of their country.[42] Rwanda has had a very hard and long pilgrimage of justice and peace. Through women working together with men, Rwanda is now moving forward; although it still has things to deal with in terms of peace and justice, the way is clear and walkable. Moreover, clergywomen played a great role in bringing justice, in peace building, and in Rwandan reconstruction. They have taken part in pastoral counselling, teaching widows to support themselves, helping orphans to build their own families, and comforting them. In this pilgrimage of justice and peace, the church may allow women clergy as much as they can and liberate them through transformative actions, because the case of Rwanda shows that women are able to achieve and change more.

Conclusion

For a long time, the church has been led by patriarchal understanding and practice that excludes and undermines women in the church's mission. But now the church has started the pilgrimage that aims to change the selfish understanding and lead the church in a world where people celebrate life together. It is clearly seen that women clergy, especially in elite positions, are influencing positive changes in the church and even in society. The challenge is that women clergy still lead very few large churches, because their capacities are still being undermined. Again, the number of women pastors in leadership positions is still low. Some denominations still exclude women from some church activities; for example, some churches cannot ordain women, even though women in church ministry perform the same activities as ordained men. Yet because she is a woman, she cannot be ordained. Therefore, the church needs to keep going on this way of liberating women and allowing them to be free participants in all areas of the church's life. The church should also stand up against any kind of discrimination and advocate for those who are on the margins because of conservative tendencies. Thus, in the church of Africa, we need to pray for women clergy, who are still discriminated against in church ministry; but the church should also take action on this issue, not only pray, because faith without works is dead. Clergywomen are also strong enough to build the kingdom of God. The God of life leads in peace, justice, and dignity.

42. Ibid.; Izabiliza, "The Role of Women in Reconstruction."

9

Gender Justice: A Mission of the Church Today

Emmanuel Kwizera

Abstract

The issue of injustice toward women was constructed in African societies even before the colonial era. Gender imbalances have been a preoccupation for churches and civil society since post-independence, but it is still a burning issue which needs to be discussed and addressed. The aim of this essay is to discover how biblical and sociocultural worldviews are contributing to gender injustice and to try to see how we can achieve gender justice in our churches. The overall objectives of this study are based on the following questions: Is it true that biblical texts, churches, and African culture contribute to injustice toward women? What is their contribution to gender and injustice toward women in Africa? Can the churches and the African context contribute today to the pilgrimage of gender justice? What is the church's contribution in discouraging gender injustice in African society? To respond to these questions, a critical and thematic exploration of secondary literature, theory, and data were used. In addition, descriptive methodology was used for the issues of gender in the Bible, in churches, and in an African context. The study proves that many women feel incapable compared to men because society has taught this for many years; it is up to society to correct its teachings and empower women. The study's findings show that the church itself should see if all men and women are treated equally in the church and in society in general. By using the authority of the Bible, the church should break down all norms and beliefs which promote inequality.

Introduction

When it comes to relations between men and women, many biblical and social interpretations exist. In some cultures, including biblical ones, a man is seen as the image of dignity and honour more than a woman is, because he preceded her in one creation story. Traditionally, in some African cultures, the man is responsible for parenting his children, looking out for the wellbeing of the members of the family, including his wife, and speaking on their behalf. The woman's concern is domestic issues: she is responsible for farming and marketing. Male superiority has been constructed for a long time by the society and the culture. For this reason, on one hand, for some cultures, women were seen as weak, incapable of rational thinking, and are not suited for leadership functions. On the other hand, some African cultures had women as leaders, such as Chewa in Malawi and Akan in Ghana.

Some cultures view the female body as weak and inferior compared to the male body. This is not merely history we are narrating: even now, in some churches and societies, women are still treated that way, such as not being allowed to be ordained as a pastor. As those who are striving for a world of justice and desiring to be one in Christ, churches and societies must take responsibility for fighting against injustices toward women which are rooted in our cultures, social constructions, and theological arenas. This essay will discuss gender justice – especially what churches, theological institutions, and civil societies must do to fight against discrimination and oppression of women. It comprises several sections: a literature review, biblical and theological foundations of gender justice, relevance of gender justice in the church, conclusion, and recommendations.

Background of the Study

In Africa, religion determined not only what people believed but how they lived and interacted with others. According to John Mbiti,[1] religion in Africa is a way of life. Since religion formatted the culture, it determines the roles to be played by the genders in religion. Togarasei (2008) states that[2] gender refers to culturally constructed differentiation between men and women in terms of expected social roles. Today, women are experiencing much injustice within churches because they are deprived of certain rights and responsibilities (p.211).

Scripture calls everyone to strive for justice – in every tribe, race, community, country, continent, and the world as whole. God sent his Son Jesus Christ to empower us to live and work together for justice (John 13:34; Heb. 12:14). But still today, in some places, men and women do not participate equally in the life of societies and churches, especially in decision-making processes. They face these challenges even though the word of liberation, justice, and love is preached all over the world. Also, women are exposed to injustice, discrimination, violence, and oppression because there are still norms, values,

---

1. Mbiti (1961:1) *African Religions and Philosophy.* New York: Preager.

2. Lovemore Tograsei and Ezra Chitando, "Teaching Religion and Gender in Contexts of HIV and AIDS in Africa," in *Mainstreaming HIV and AIDS in Theological Education: Experiences and Exportations,* ed. Ezra Chitando (Geneva: WCC Publications, 2008), 211–23, at 214.

social conditions, and beliefs that discriminate against them.

Despite various efforts in societies, churches, and other organizations, there is still an unfair division of gender roles. There are different opinions on why this inequality in gender practices persists.

Although society and the church have discriminated against women, many people do not want to talk about it. They use ideas from their cultures and texts from the Bible which they say support their wrongdoing. Benoit Girardin notes that in many countries, a kind of silent discrimination can be observed whereby money-yielding activities are entrusted to men, while women remain tied to subsistence and bartering.[3] He confirms that in some countries, in the education sector, girls' attendance decreases much more than that of boys. Yet, according to research by the British Aid Agency, a 1% increase in the number of girls with secondary schooling boosts growth in annual income by 0.3% in many counties. This shows that women and girls, if they are empowered, play a key role in development. In addition, what James Emman Kwegyir Aggrey of Ghana said about the education of boys and girls has become an African proverb: If you educate a man, you educate an individual, but if you educate a woman, you educate a whole nation.

Many people wonder why discrimination and gender injustice continue today. The aim of this essay is to discover how biblical and sociocultural worldviews contribute to gender injustice and to try to see how we can achieve gender justice in our churches. A descriptive methodology was used to explore the issues of gender in the Bible, in churches, and in an African context by seeing how various scholars comment on this issue.

The overall objectives are based on the following questions:

- Is it true that biblical texts, churches, and African culture contribute to injustice toward women? What is their contribution to gender and injustice toward women in Africa?
- Can the churches and the African context contribute today to the pilgrimage of gender justice? What is the church's contribution in discouraging gender injustice in African society?

---

3. Benoit Girardin, *Family, Gender and Community Development* (Butare: PIASS, 2013), 17.

Literature Review

Global Views on Gender Justice

The term "gender" refers to socially constructed roles associated with biological sex in a given context. According to Vicki S. Helgeson, gender refers to the expectations that go along with male versus female. It also refers to sexual orientation and the diverse ways in which people express their gender identity.[4] In some tribes, churches, and societies, men are valued more than women.

The term "justice" is the state of being just and fair in a certain circumstance. When we speak of gender justice, we refer to men and women having the same value, opportunities, rights, and obligations in all aspects of life. Margot A. Hurlbert points out that justice includes fairness, equality, and moral righteousness.[5] It overcomes social exclusion or oppression of individuals and groups, including that which is based on gender, social class, racial-ethnic identity, cultural practices, religious belief, sexual orientation, or disability.

Gender justice is the state where men and women are treated equally. There is no marginalization and exclusion because of gender. Both genders have equal rights and opportunities. According to a 2012 World Bank report, gender injustice leads to poverty and suffering.[6] In the church, gender justice means welcoming people of different genders as children of God in an inclusive way. They should be invited into the fellowship of God and share together in the blessings of God. The church must be open to all.

According to Karl Barth, as quoted by theologian Mary Daly, most people consider that a woman's task and function is to actualize and assume the responsibilities assigned by her husband.[7] The church fathers said that a man is the real human being.[8] The woman must help the man primarily by bearing his children. She is a secondary creature, as she belongs to her husband. These views of persons and these descriptions of women have led to gender injustices; as a result, women suffer. In some cultures and churches, women are not welcome to assume certain leadership responsibilities; they are blocked due to patriarchal gender roles.

---

4. Helgeson (2009:4). *The Psychology of Gender. Pearson.*

5. Hurlbert, c.M. and Blitz, M. (1996:19). *Composition and Resistance.*

6. World Bank report (2012:17). *Report on Justice.*

7. Mary Daly, *Beyond God the Father* (Boston: Beacon Press, 1973), 202.

8. Abel Isaksson, *Marriage and Ministry in the New Temple* (Copenhagen: Munksgaard, 1969), 3.

In some contexts, women are oppressed in their family and are not informed of or involved in the family's financial management. This causes conflict between husbands and wives. Some women run away from their homes; others seek a divorce from their partner. Those who persevere and continue to live under those injustices feel ashamed, hopeless, and traumatized. Tharcisse Gatwa states that the violence against women affects their children and future generations.[9] Gatwa believes there must be theological interventions and Christian models which lead to gender justice and equity.

Patriarchal systems and toxic masculinity have worked against women and have prevented them from effectively integrating on the global stage. However, there have been some changes in the churches and in our contemporary society. For instance, in some churches – though not all – women are assuming more leadership responsibilities than before. This is much appreciated. In other contexts, women are not allowed to be pastor, are neglected, and experience discrimination. This is a global issue which undermines the abundant life of women. Society and the churches must not keep quiet about this issue, because it wounds the world in general.

African Worldview on Gender Justice

In African societies, as in other societies, women's human rights are mostly neglected. In the past in Rwanda, women were not allowed to study the sciences. It is only recently that women can study science and compete for political positions at a national and even an international level. It is common in some African countries to find more young men than women in institutions of higher learning, even though there are more women than men in many societies.[10] This happens because it is believed that women do not need to develop their minds to the same level as men. In addition, some cultures in Africa see girls as visitors in the family, because somebody will take her after she grows up; this distorted view leads some parents not to educate their daughters. Christian families, churches, and Africa in general must fight against this false understanding. According to Douglas Wanjohi,[11] the proclamation and application of the liberating gospel should help Africans to move toward full liberation. While the roles of each gender are recognized,

---

9. G. Tharcisse, *Violence and Conflict Management in Families and Communities* (Butare: PIASS, 2014), 37.

10. Douglas Wanjohi Waruta, ed., *Caring and Sharing: Pastoral Counselling in the African Perspective* (Nairobi: Uzima, 1995), 62.

11. Ibid., 63.

full opportunities for growth and development should be provided for both genders; allowing one gender to dominate the other is unbiblical, because man and woman are equal before God since creation (Gen. 1:27). Also, the news from the World Council of Churches in September 2019 shows that women and girls in South Africa are still discriminated against, raped, and killed without any reason.[12] But it also describes how female church leaders and theologians from the Dutch Reformed Church have brought out a strong statement challenging patriarchal and unhealthy theologies that target women.[13] The statement calls patriarchy within the church a "disease of the soul" that directly contradicts the gospel of Jesus.[14] Furthermore, in Rwanda, the number of women who become pregnant when they are still young and do not have the means for themselves and their babies to survive is still high. Rwandan news reported that in Gatsibo, a district in the Eastern Province, 680 young women became pregnant within an 18-month period in 2019[15] These examples show how women in Africa are suffering in different ways.

For these current examples, the church should advocate for women and challenge all kinds of injustices toward them.

The Church Fathers and Reformers Views on Gender

The church fathers had different understandings of women. According to Clark, women were responsible for sin as the root of all evil because of the disobedience of Eve, which resulted in death for human beings.[16] They tried to show the infamous women who are remembered for their negative actions toward men, such as Delilah, Jezebel, and Bathsheba. Sawyer identifies arguments which show that the church fathers did not consider women as equal to men.[17]

First, women were viewed as the second sex because Eve was created after Adam; also, because she was disobedient, they believed she does not represent the image of God. Second, they blamed Eve as the one who introduced the sin into the world. Two biblical passages, 2 Corinthians 11:3 and 1 Timothy 2:14, were used to support their views that women must be subordinate and inferior to men within the church. Tertullian argued that women were not

---

12. WCC weekly news, September 2019.

13. Ibid.

14. Ibid.

15. Minister of health report in her speech at Gatsibo district on 24-5-2019, from Igihe.com

16. Elizabeth A. Clark, "Ideology, History, and the Construction of "Woman" in Late Ancient Christianity, *Journal of Early Christian Studies* 2: 2 (1994), 155–84, at 168.

17. Deborah F. Sawyer, *Women and Religion in the First Christian Centuries* (London: Routledge, 1996), 149.

permitted to speak in the church, to teach, to baptize, to sacrifice, or to fulfil any other male responsibilities. He saw women as the "devil's gateway, and the root of all sin."[18]

Augustine, meanwhile, said that women must be suppressed and kept in check, and their physical and social mobility restricted, because they do not possess of God's image.[19] For Thomas Aquinas, women are incomplete or imperfect in body, will, and reason. They are a necessary evil or imperfection in nature.

The Protestant Reformation began in 1517 with Luther, who challenged the custom of selling indulgences.[20] The Reformation was a reaction against the abuse of power, corruption, and the deception of common people by the pope and, by implication, of the Catholic Church. The Reformers' opinions differed somewhat from those of the Church fathers, as Martin Luther and John Calvin believed that men and women were created as equals. In Lyndal Roper's view, not only did the Reformers view men and women as equals, but also they involved women in the Reformation process.[21]

Even if the church fathers neglected women and saw them as evil, God recognizes, respects, and directs gender roles equally. Jesus Christ also truly put into practice the vision of God. Human beings have used their own biases and prejudices to create inequality between men and women. As young theologians and scholars of the day, we must join hands to overcome this issue of gender injustice.

Biblical and Theological Foundations of Gender Justice

Gender Justice in the Old Testament

The accounts of the creation of man and woman in Genesis (1:27-28 and even 2:18-24) say, "So God created man in his image, in the image of God he created him, male and female he created them." In the Old Testament, not only women did not receive the covenant of circumcision, but also they could not function as leaders of the household in most tribes. These practices ledKoehler to conclude that the Old Testament discriminated against

18. Elisabeth Schüssler Fiorenza, *In Memory of Her: A Feminist Theological Reconstruction of Christian Origins* (New York: Crossroad, 1990), 54–55.

19. Ruether 1985:67). *Woman guides: Readings Towards a Feminist Theology.*

20. Mary T. Malone, *Women and Christianity: Vol. I: The First Thousand Years* (Maryknoll: Orbis, 2001), 35.

21. Roper (290–301). *The Holy Household: Women and Morals in Reformation Augsburg*

women.[22] He says that the covenant is with men; women had no place in this revelation. Obogunrin, however, did not agree with this view: he said that the community of God includes the family no matter their age or their sex.[23] Women not only share with men in the blessings and responsibilities of the covenant, but they were also vital to the fulfilment of its blessings, which included long life, prosperity, children, and land (Deut. 5:29-33). Women shared equally with men in the blessing of worship by resting on the Sabbath (Ex. 20:10), listening to the reading of the law (Deut. 31:9-13), and rejoicing before the Lord.

The mission of God in this world includes men and women. In both the Old and New Testaments, men and women were ministers. For instance, Myriam the prophetess (Ex. 15:20) worked with Aaron and Moses in the service of God. Deborah was both a political and a religious leader.

Gender Justice in the New Testament

Jesus himself had male and female disciples (Luke 8:2-3). Some of the women shared their economic resources. Several of these women were the first witnesses to the resurrection (Luke 24:22). In Romans 16, women are mentioned working in different functions and ministries, including working with Paul, such as Prisca (Rom. 16:3) and apostles like Junia (Rom. 16:7). Some women also assumed different responsibilities in Christian communities in the first century. In the history of the church, some women suffered from persecution because of their witness to Christ as well.

Jesus' treatment of women is revolutionary in many ways. Even though the Jewish religion said that men and women were created in God's image and had the same value, women were treated as inferior to men in the society. Victor Paul states that women were not allowed to testify in court trials; they could not go out in public or talk to foreigners.[24] The Sanhedrin, which had the juridical and religious power, was made up of 70 to 72 men. The three main Jewish religious groups – the Essenes, the Pharisees, and the Sadducees – all kept up the laws and social conventions that were dominated by men. Women were not counted. For example, when Jesus feeds a great crowd (Matt.14:13-21), the women are not counted. The way Jesus treated women shocked some Jews and caused conflict.

____

22. Ludwig Koehler, *Old Testament Theology* (London: Westminster Press, 1975), 69.

23. Obogunrin (2006:17). *New Testament Textual and Literary Criticism.*

24. Victor Paul Furnish, "Women in the Church," in *The Moral Teaching of Paul: Selected Issues,* rev. ed. (Nashville: Abingdon Press, 1985), 83–114.

Jesus showed no discrimination but treated women and men as equals. He violated a number of Old Testament regulations which specified gender inequality. He refused to follow the behavioural rules established by the Jewish religious groups of the day.

The encounters of Jesus with women show not only his respect but also his appreciation for them. According to David W. Kling, women were visible and active not only in the ministry of Jesus, but also in the life of the apostolic church.[25] Women joined the church, expanding its numbers. Acts 5:14 records that "more than ever believers were added to the Lord, great numbers of both men and women."

The Churches' View on Gender Justice

Most of the churches agree that men and women are created equal in the image of God. They refer to Genesis 1:27: "God created humankind in his image, in the image of God he created them; male and female he created them." As recorded in the Bible, women are involved in church responsibilities and leadership. However, there is a still gap in some churches which prevent women from taking on responsibilities. Kwame Bediako says that the church cannot exclude women in its functional operations.[26] Any church which attempts this is not faithful. Aylward Shorter states that the churches in Africa should encourage all their members – men and women – to participate in the mission that they were assigned by God.[27] There should be no discrimination based on gender.

Currently, even if some churches do discriminate against women, they are appreciated for the roles they do play. Some churches ordain women as pastors; others have women at the top level of leadership. For example, in the Presbyterian Church of Rwanda, 30 percent of those in pastoral ministry are ordained women, and some have leadership duties in the church: the deputy and vice president of the church is a woman. There are women who are doing theological studies which prepare them to be ministers in the church. This shows that the Presbyterian Church of Rwanda promotes gender equality at all levels.

---

25. David W. Kling, "'One in Christ Jesus': Women's Ministry and Ordination," in *The Bible in History: How the Texts Have Shaped the Times* (Oxford: Oxford University Press, 2004), 269–94.

26. Kwame Bediako, *African Journal of Biblical Studies*: Christianity in Africa (2005:70),

27. Aylward Shorter, *Christian Family Power in Africa* (Kenya: Nakuru Press, 1977).

According to national, regional, and international gender policy instruments, the Presbyterian Church of Rwanda fights all forms of discrimination, such as

- stereotyping and unequal power relations between men and women, and boys and girls
- gender-based exclusion and discrimination
- family violence for women and men, boys and girls
- injustice based on gender balance
- discrimination of women and girls based on the misinterpretation of the Bible.

Due to the cultural and historical gender norms in society, many barriers to gender equality among men and women still exist in some churches. This includes some beliefs that are based on interpretations of the Bible and a broader misunderstanding or misinterpretation of the Bible regarding women's role in the household and in society. The churches are called to be committed to combating these strongly held cultural beliefs and gender norms and to apply gender awareness training through their training centres. They should target couples and families through parishes, training centres, programmes, and women's and family departments.

The Relevance of Gender Justice in the Church

One purpose of the church is to ensure that gender equity and equality are integrated, promoted, and accounted for at institutional, programme, and community levels. This includes internally as an organization and in interactions with stakeholders and beneficiaries. The church should intend to lead by example in its work, including in its commitment to promote dignity and human rights for girls, women, men, and boys. In addition to the provisions outlined here, the church must be committed to confronting and challenging gender discrimination, stereotypes, and unequal power relations between men and women and boys and girls.

Aylward Shorter agrees that if there is gender justice in the church, it grows and the kingdom of God reigns.[28] Gender justice in the church promotes equal representation and participation of both men and women in all of the church's decision making.

---

28. Ibid., 7.

The practice of gender justice in the church also helps to mobilize human and financial resources to meet its goals. It serves to reinforce Christian values such as love, unity, dialogue, truth, and equality. Margaret Gallagher confirms that if the church treat women and men as equals, this could reduce the high number of women who are infected by HIV.[29] Most women become infected because their husbands force them to have sexual relations without protection. In most cultures, women do not have a say even about sexual intercourse.

Gender justice within the church promotes the welfare of families. Men and women can enjoy their life because they share their responsibilities equally and complement each other. The family is the foundation of the church and the country. Its development and fragility can affect the church. If women and men are strong and are welcomed into the church at an equal level, the church will grow.

Today, churches and civil societies are called to allow women and men to exercise their gifts equally in their homes, in the church, and in society.

Gender Justice: A Mission of Churches Today

According to Dale Robbins, churches have multiple tasks and functions.[30] Their mandate is to proclaim the gospel throughout the world and make disciples of all people (Matt. 28:19-20). They have the task of serving as a community of worship and fellowship to manifest the presence and love of Jesus. As Jesus said, "For where two or three are gathered together in my name, I am there among them" (Matt. 18:20). Therefore, the Church must nurture believers and prepare them to perform works of ministry.

The church should make sure that all kinds of people, men and women, are participating in its mission of togetherness. The issue of submission in our churches is crucial. The interpretation of Ephesians 5:21-25 provokes much discussion. Some people think that to be "a head" means to exercise power and authority; some husbands have used this passage to force their wives and other family members to bow down to serve them. This understanding must change through training the couple to understand the word of God as it was intended. In some African traditions, husbands have the right to give orders and to force their wives to do certain things. Churches and faith-based organizations have an essential role to play in challenging the prejudices that are

---

29. Gallagher (1997:17). *Becoming Aware: Human Rights and the Family.* UNESCO.
30. Robbins (1990:215). *What people ask about Church.* Victorious publications. Nashville.

profoundly embedded in cultures and traditions.

To be "a head" in the family means that the man initiates love and wellbeing for his wife and family. This is contrary to a man using power to force others in the family or to use violence to get what he wants. Like Christ, a man should try to show love and kindness and even give his life for those he loves (Eph. 5:33).

Gender justice must be seen in the unity between men and women. They should try to share the responsibilities of leadership on the basis of gifts, expertise, and availability. Gender justice covers the practice of humility and love between men and women. It is also a willingness to listen to each other and a readiness to share responsibilities.

Therefore, the church should create safe spaces for women, men, girls, and boys to prevent violence against women and gender-based violence. This can be accompanied by upholding values of dignity and justice, inclusiveness and participation.

Today women are productive; they protect the family the way men used to say it was their own responsibility to do. There should be equality and justice when it comes to responsibilities and sharing resources and income in the family.

Conclusion

Today in Rwanda, the churches are revisiting biblical and cultural interpretations of gender justice. Based on the principle of equality are the characteristics of human rights, which state that human rights are equal; there is none who is higher than another. This does not contradict Martin Luther and John Calvin, who believed that men and women were created as equals. This approach is truly biblical, as we see in Genesis 1:27.

Affirmative action means that gender-equal access to education and equal access to leadership positions in both government and churches must be encouraged. Addressing gender inequalities in the media and in public discourse is another step. Churches, theological institutions, and private institutions should have gender commissions to encourage change, advise, and challenge gender injustice from within. There is also a need for biblical hermeneutics to be taught by Christians.

Gender justice within the church promotes the welfare of families, where men and women share responsibilities equally and complement each other. The family is the foundation of the church; when families are fragile, this affects the church.

Gender justice should be understood as efforts to promote full participation by both males and females. In general, issues of gender in families, churches, and private institutions should be discussed, because the things that are hindering women's full participation in those institutions is not biological but theological, political, cultural, and social. The church should take the step to provide equal chances to both men and women through education, because both form the body of Christ.

Recommendations

After analyzing the problems of injustice and discrimination faced by women, the following recommendations are formulated for the churches and for society to achieve gender justice and peace in our communities. These are recommendations for the Africa we pray for.

- Gender injustice is a social construct: it needs to be deconstructed and reconstructed to provide equal chances to men and women. This will happen through education.
- The church should take into consideration the issue of gender injustice and try to find solutions for it by reformulating its teachings that exclude women from God's blessings.
- African pastors must offer teaching to couples before and after their wedding so they can share responsibilities and complement each other in their household once they are married.
- All churches in Africa should have gender policies and implementation plans for these policies.

10

Implication des jeunes femmes et des filles
dans les dialogues de paix au niveau international

Agnim Valery Bitchatou

Résumé

Il n'y a pas de développement sans paix et aucune paix ne peut être durable si elle n'est pas soutenue par le développement. Si la guerre est souvent l'affaire des hommes, la paix est plutôt celle des femmes. Ce n'est peut-être pas systématique, mais l'expérience montre cependant que la discussion et la médiation permettent parfois à des femmes appartenant à des groupes rivaux en conflit de trouver plus facilement un terrain d'entente. Elles sont donc une force pour la paix et la réconciliation.

La participation des jeunes femmes et des filles à la consolidation de la paix permettra d'instaurer une paix durable

Des conflits font rage dans la plupart des pays africains depuis des siècles. Conflits entre fils et filles de même nation, conflits entre clans. Beaucoup d'initiatives ont été prises par nos gouvernants pour instaurer la paix sur le continent africain.

Il est primordial que les femmes participent au processus de paix et à la consolidation de la paix, car elles sont particulièrement touchées par les conflits.

Situation particulière des femmes dans les conflits armés

Dans les conflits armés, les femmes et les jeunes filles sont souvent victimes de violences sexuelles et humiliations. Elles sont contraintes de se livrer à la prostitution ou connaissent une grossesse non voulue. À cela s'ajoute le risque de contamination des maladies sexuellement transmissibles. Elles voient disparaître leurs maris et leurs enfants et doivent assumer la charge de leur famille.

Dans les situations de guerre ou de conflit violent, la répartition inégale des ressources, les agissements illégaux et le mépris du droit humanitaire international pèsent lourdement sur les femmes et les jeunes filles. Celles-ci sont particulièrement touchées dans un certain nombre de pays africains dévastés par la guerre où les droits de la personne sont bafoués et où les violences liées au genre sont légion.

Les conflits violents, avec les déstabilisations, les déplacements de populations et les destructions d'infrastructures qui les accompagnent, ont sur les populations touchées des effets différents selon leur genre. En outre, l'exil forcé et l'exode de compétences qui s'ensuit entravent le développement socioéconomique du continent africain. L'étendue et la nature exactes des injustices et des crimes contre l'humanité qui sont liés au genre, ainsi que la perte de ressources humaines, demandent à être évaluées précisément.

Point n'est besoin de s'étendre sur la vulnérabilité des femmes africaines face aux conflits armés. Les crimes auxquels les femmes sont constamment soumises sont connus, même s'ils ne défraient pas les médias. Ces crimes de haine sont le reflet de la négation de la femme en tant que sujet politique. La guerre ne fait que dévoiler grossièrement le prolongement de la tyrannie et de la discrimination que les femmes et les jeunes filles subissent dans leurs familles et communautés en temps de paix.

Mais lorsque les protagonistes d'un conflit se réunissent, la gent féminine ne fait guère partie de leurs préoccupations. Les questions qui les concernent et celles liées au genre ne figurent pas en tête de l'ordre du jour. Et lorsque la situation des femmes est évoquée, ce sont toujours des femmes âgées qui prennent la parole. Or, les jeunes femmes et jeunes filles, font face à de grandes difficultés, mais elles ne sont pas prises en compte. Elles s'entendent dire: « Vous êtes jeunes, qu'est-ce que vous y connaissez?» Les programmes d'action des jeunes pour la paix et la sécurité n'incluant pas toujours des femmes, les jeunes femmes restent invisibles. Ces programmes sont dirigés par des hommes qui ne leur accordent aucune place.

Les femmes: la paix et la sécurité

Pour instaurer une paix durable, nous avons besoin des voix des femmes ou des féministes. Depuis la prévention et la résolution des conflits jusqu'aux processus de réconciliation et de relèvement économique après un conflit, on observe que la participation significative des femmes dans les processus de paix augmente les chances de réussite de près de 35%. Mais cette participation ne doit pas se limiter à leur représentation et à des quotas. Une participation significative implique que les femmes s'asseyent à la table des négociations, que leurs intérêts et leur vécu soient pleinement reflétés dans les processus de paix et qu'elles soient prises en compte dans les initiatives de relèvement au lendemain d'un conflit.

Pendant la guerre civile guatémaltèque qui a duré 36 ans, dans un petit village à proximité de l'avant-poste de Sepur Zarco, les femmes autochtones ont été systématiquement violées et réduites en esclavage par les militaires. Ce qui leur est arrivé n'est pas exceptionnel, mais ce qui s'est passé ensuite a changé l'Histoire. Entre 2011 et 2016, 15 survivantes se sont battues pour obtenir justice devant la Cour suprême du Guatemala. À l'issue de ce procès sans précédent, deux anciens officiers militaires ont été condamnés pour crimes contre l'humanité et 18 mesures de réparation ont été prononcées en faveur des survivantes et de leur village. Les abuelas de Sepur Zarco, un terme respectueux pour désigner ces femmes, attendent maintenant que justice soit rendue. Pour elles, obtenir justice signifie notamment assurer l'éducation des enfants de leur village, avoir accès à la terre et à un établissement de santé, mais aussi mettre en œuvre d'autres mesures similaires pour mettre fin à la pauvreté abjecte dont leur village souffre depuis des générations. La justice doit être vécue.

I. Les femmes, principales victimes des conflits armés

Les femmes sont souvent les principales victimes des conflits armés, au titre notamment des violences sexuelles. L'ONU estime qu'entre 100 000 et 250 000 femmes ont été violées pendant les trois mois du génocide rwandais en 1994, et que les milices armées ont violé plus de 60 000 femmes pendant la guerre civile en Sierra Leone et plus de 40 000 pendant le conflit au Libéria. Bien souvent, les femmes ont moins de chances que les hommes de reprendre une vie normale, d'obtenir justice pour les violations de leurs droits fondamentaux et de contribuer à la réforme des lois et des institutions publiques après un conflit. De plus, elles sont très souvent tenues à l'écart des négociations de paix et des processus de reconstruction.

La Résolution 1325 de l'ONU

Depuis 2000, *le Conseil de sécurité de l'ONU* a adopté sept résolutions sur le thème « Femmes, paix et sécurité », centrées sur la place des femmes dans la construction de la paix, la reconstruction et la lutte contre les violences spécifiques dont elles peuvent être victimes en temps de guerre. La résolution 1325, adoptée le 31 octobre 2000, est la première résolution à établir le lien entre les femmes et la paix et la sécurité. Elle reconnaît que les femmes sont touchées de manière disproportionnée par les conflits du fait de l'impact particulier des violences sexuelles.

En outre, dans la résolution 1325, le Conseil de sécurité :

◊ « Demande instamment aux États Membres de faire en sorte que les femmes soient davantage représentées à tous les niveaux de prise de décisions dans les institutions et mécanismes nationaux, régionaux et internationaux pour la prévention, la gestion et le règlement des différends » (paragr. 1) ;

◊ « Demande à toutes les parties à un conflit armé de prendre des mesures particulières pour protéger les femmes et les petites filles contre les actes de violence sexiste, en particulier le viol et les autres formes de sévices sexuels, ainsi que contre toutes les autres formes de violence dans les situations de conflit armé » (paragr. 10).

Des exemples d'implications des femmes dans les processus de paix

De 1998 à 2003 s'est tenue la deuxième guerre du Congo en République Démocratique du Congo (RDC). Ce conflit qui a impliqué neuf États africains reste la plus grande guerre interétatique de l'histoire de l'Afrique contemporaine. Selon les Nations Unies, plus de 200 000 femmes ont souffert de violences sexuelles depuis 1998. Lors du processus de paix appelé « Dialogue inter congolais», qui a conduit à la signature de «l'Accord global et inclusif» le 17 décembre 2002, il y avait 43 femmes impliquées contre 300 hommes. La faible représentativité des femmes s'expliquerait par le fait que le médiateur ait cherché en premier lieu à ressembler les personnes, principalement des hommes, directement impliquées dans le conflit. Leur exclusion a poussé les femmes à mettre en place une stratégie alternative consistant à associer des expertes à des femmes membres des délégations officielles. Ainsi, elles ont réussi à mettre en place des actions communes et des initiatives de lobbying afin de faire aboutir les objectifs fixés à l'occasion du « Dialogue inter congolais» et surtout de prendre position lorsqu'il y a eu des blocages dans les négociations.

Entre 1989 et 1996 et entre 2000 et 2003, le Libéria a connu deux guerres civiles. Les femmes ont joué un rôle important dans la résolution de ces conflits, notamment par l'intermédiaire d'organisations de la société civile. Plusieurs organisations de femmes telles que l'AFELL (*Association of Female Liberian Lawyers*) et le MARWOPNET (*Mano River Women's Peace Network*) ont manifesté activement contre les différents groupes armés. L'AFELL a réalisé un travail considérable sur la reconnaissance du viol comme arme de guerre. L'association a d'ailleurs été autorisée à poursuivre les auteurs d'agressions sexuelles commises pendant les conflits. L'une des illustrations les plus significatives de l'autonomisation des femmes à la fin de la seconde guerre civile est l'élection, en novembre 2005, d'Ellen Johnson-Sirleaf à la tête du Libéria. Elle est devenue la première cheffe d'État africaine.

Au vu de tout ceci, une question demeure.

Pourquoi impliquer les femmes dans le processus de consolidation de la paix?

La paix et le développement sont étroitement liés : il n'y a pas de développement sans paix et aucune paix ne peut être durable si elle n'est pas soutenue par le développement. On ne peut pas construire une paix durable en oubliant une grande partie de la population. Si la guerre est souvent l'affaire des hommes, la paix est plutôt celle des femmes. Ce n'est peut-être pas systématique, mais l'expérience montre, cependant, que la discussion et la médiation permettent parfois à des femmes appartenant à des groupes rivaux en conflit de trouver plus facilement un terrain d'entente. Elles sont donc une force pour la paix et la réconciliation et doivent être mieux intégrées dans les processus de paix.

La prévention des conflits armés demeure le meilleur paramètre de la paix et de la sécurité en Afrique. Construire la paix, c'est prévenir la guerre. Les femmes ont un rôle décisif à jouer dans la promotion de la tolérance et de la non-violence, car elles sont la première école de la vie. Elles peuvent manifester leur influence d'épouses en faisant régner l'intégrité et la respectabilité dans leur foyer. Elles peuvent également associer leurs frères et sœurs au mouvement de la paix en organisant des formations, des séminaires et des campagnes de sensibilisation.

Dans tous les pays des Grands Lacs, les femmes constituent la grande majorité de la population. Dans certaines régions, elles sont restées seules après les guerres. Il est tout naturel de dire que la femme donne la vie et qu'elle est la mieux placée pour en connaître la valeur et pour mieux la préserver.

Les exemples positifs montrent que, de manière générale, les femmes participent activement aux mouvements en faveur de la paix, aussi bien au sein d'organisations féminines dans leur pays qu'à l'extérieur de ce dernier. Les femmes ont souvent bénéficié d'une autorité morale en raison de leur rôle de mère.

En 1996 et 1997, les violences qui éclatent à Bangui révèlent à la population centrafricaine que la paix n'est pas un acquis naturel, mais une valeur à la fois politique et culturelle à conquérir et à consolider au quotidien. Dès les premières manifestations de violence, les Centrafricaines se sont spontanément mobilisées pour rechercher une solution pacifique. Cette intervention des femmes en faveur de la paix n'est pas un fait nouveau dans le pays. Chaque fois que l'harmonie sociale et la vie humaine ont été menacées, les Centrafricaines ont constitué un ultime rempart contre la folie meurtrière des hommes.

Les Rwandaises et les Burundais ont bien compris que dans une société traumatisée par la guerre, la division et le génocide, elles pouvaient mener, de par leur rôle social, de petites actions permettant de comprendre la douleur de l'autre et de se lever pour réparer les pots cassés par le conflit opposant leurs maris, leurs fils ou leurs frères.

En juillet 1998, 17 partis politiques différents réunis à Arusha, en Tanzanie, ont entamé des pourparlers de paix afin de résoudre le conflit sévissant au Burundi. Aucun organisme civil n'a été autorisé à participer à ces négociations et parmi les 126 délégués officiels, on ne comptait que deux (2) femmes.

À Bukavu, les Congolaises ont su exprimer leurs griefs et leur opposition à la guerre du fait même de leur rôle de mère, alors que les autorités interdisaient toute autre forme de protestation. Les femmes congolaises sont très actives même au sein de la diaspora pour exiger d'être entendues dans le processus de négociation de la paix et de reconstruction du pays.

Au Rwanda, après le génocide, les femmes ont été les premières à s'entraider et à oser partager leurs terribles expériences. Tout commence par-là: il faut oser en parler. Plus tard, quand les femmes réfugiées hutues sont rentrées des camps, certaines organisations de femmes ont organisé un accueil de solidarité spontané sans considération d'ethnie. Cela n'exclut évidemment pas les haines qui subsistent, mais ces quelques actions positives ont montré qu'il était possible de vivre ensemble et de construire l'avenir.

Au Soudan et au Libéria, les femmes ont figuré au rang d'observatrices durant les négociations de paix.

Sur le plan international, les dirigeantes de 7 pays d'Afrique ont lancé l'initiative « Partners in peace » pour demander la mise en œuvre des accords de Lusaka et offrir aux femmes la possibilité d'être intégrées dans le processus de paix. Elles ont publié une déclaration pour la paix et se sont retrouvées en septembre 2000.

Le Programme d'action de la quatrième Conférence des Nations Unies sur les femmes (Beijing, 1995) dit ceci : « S'il est vrai que les communautés subissent tout entières les conséquences des conflits armés et du terrorisme, les femmes et les petites filles sont particulièrement touchées en raison de leur place dans la société et de leur sexe » (paragr. 135).

En octobre 2000, le Conseil de sécurité des Nations Unies a adopté une résolution innovatrice (1325) qui reconnaît que le maintien et la promotion de la paix et de la sécurité exigent la participation des femmes aux prises de décisions, et il a appelé tous les acteurs à adopter une perspective tenant compte de cet élément. Cette résolution demandait en même temps au Secrétaire général Kofi Annan d'augmenter le nombre de femmes parmi ses envoyées spéciales à travers le monde,

La communauté internationale reconnaît donc qu'il faut accroître la participation des femmes au règlement des conflits et tenir compte de la problématique homme-femme dans l'ensemble des analyses, politiques et programmes conçus pour venir à bout des conflits et instaurer la paix. Mais, sur le plan individuel, les organismes ne savent pas toujours comment traduire ce consensus international en mesures concrètes. La nature et les causes des crises politiques africaines, la persistance des structures qui maintiennent la femme africaine dans un statut de subordonnée et la faible adhésion mondiale à l'égalité de fait entre l'homme et la femme rendent impossible l'édification d'une paix durable.

Les crises africaines sont, entre autres, le reflet de l'abandon du monde rural naguère porté par l'agriculture de subsistance, au profit d'une conception du développement axée sur le commerce et les services. Ne l'oublions jamais, l'Afrique est un monde profondément rural. C'est dans ce monde agricole porté à bout de bras par les femmes que l'on trouve la majeure partie des victimes de la guerre. Prévenir la guerre, c'est renouer avec les politiques de la ruralité : accroître le financement de l'agriculture, développer le soutien aux femmes rurales, renforcer la capacité de production, etc.

La paix commence par soi-même, et généralement on donne ce qu'on a. Si une femme n'a pas de paix dans son cœur, elle ne peut pas en donner. L'expérience montre cependant que les femmes retrouvent la paix intérieure plus rapidement que les hommes. Il faut aider les femmes à retrouver cette paix intérieure pour qu'elles soient en mesure de la donner aux autres.

Comment mieux impliquer les femmes et les jeunes filles dans le processus de paix ?

Parmi la panoplie de solutions possibles, nous avons formulé une recommandation en dix points que voici :

1. Appuyer la participation des femmes et des jeunes filles aux négociations de paix, car les femmes rencontrent beaucoup d'opposition quand il s'agit de participer aux négociations de paix officielles ;

2. Accroître la participation des femmes et des jeunes filles aux règlements de conflits et à l'élaboration des décisions, notamment en nommant des femmes à des postes décisionnaires liés aux négociations de paix et à la réconciliation nationale ;

3. Former les femmes et les jeunes filles aux techniques de négociation ;

4. Rendre l'éducation plus juste et plus ouverte aux filles : le renforcement des capacités des filles par l'éducation est une nécessité. Il conviendrait de mettre en place des politiques leur permettant de fréquenter l'enseignement secondaire en plus grand nombre et de poursuivre leurs études jusqu'à leur terme. À cela devraient s'ajouter des programmes leur donnant les moyens et la confiance nécessaires pour propager une culture de la paix ;

5. Favoriser le développement d'environnements sociaux, politiques et culturels qui soutiennent les efforts des femmes en matière de paix et permettent de garantir des acquis durables en faveur de l'égalité des genres ;

6. Renforcer le pouvoir économique des femmes et développer des politiques au profit des jeunes filles en élargissant les possibilités qu'elles ont d'accéder à des crédits ou prêts, à des postes décisionnels, à la gestion des affaires publiques et à l'information ;

7. Sensibiliser le personnel militaire féminin et les épouses d'officiers en les encourageant à jouer un rôle actif dans la prévention des conflits et en les mettant en relation avec les activités organisées en matière de construction de la paix ;

8. Prôner le désarmement et demander aux gouvernements de réduire les dépenses militaires et de réaffecter les ressources ainsi dégagées

à l'éducation en général et à une culture de la paix en particulier ;

9. Amener tous les types de médias à s'engager pleinement en faveur du développement et de l'avancement des femmes et des jeunes filles, et encourager les artistes et les journalistes à contribuer à promouvoir la culture de la paix ;

10. Mettre en place des initiatives ciblées visant à renforcer les capacités et le pouvoir de la société civile.

La société civile a un très grand rôle à jouer dans la construction de la démocratie et le respect des droits de la personne. Bien que limitées, les organisations de femmes s'avèrent être des lieux privilégiés offrant des possibilités et des occasions d'acquérir et de développer des compétences, des connaissances et des ressources. Ces organisations se mobilisent, agissent auprès des pouvoirs publics et mènent des campagnes contre la violence, les lois injustes et oppressives, la pauvreté et la maltraitance familiale. Ces activités contribuent considérablement à la paix. Grâce à elles, les femmes affirment leur détermination à lutter contre les guerres et les violences de toutes sortes, et elles proposent des solutions.

La communauté internationale reconnaît aujourd'hui les contributions capitales des femmes dans les processus de construction de la paix. On peut remarquer l'intention de la communauté internationale d'inclure systématiquement et de façon significative les femmes dans la prévention et la résolution des conflits et dans la reconstruction post-conflit, mais aussi de les considérer comme des partenaires à part entière dans les processus formels et informels de résolution des conflits et de négociation de la paix.

Des études confirment les rôles essentiels et déterminants qu'ont joués et que peuvent jouer les femmes du Burundi, du Cameroun, de la République centrafricaine, de Namibie, de Tanzanie et de Somalie dans la prévention et la résolution des conflits comme dans la promotion d'une culture de la paix, en s'appuyant sur des méthodes traditionnelles.

L'Afrique subsaharienne ne s'illustre pas uniquement comme étant l'entité géographique mondiale la plus affectée par l'extrême pauvreté. Elle est aussi la région mondiale la plus touchée par la guerre.

La féminisation de la pauvreté et de la violence consécutive aux conflits armés devrait conduire la communauté internationale ainsi que les nations africaines à repenser la paix et la sécurité selon une perspective féministe.

Il faut redéfinir les paramètres de la paix, en tablant davantage sur la prévention que sur la résolution des conflits, en faisant preuve d'une meilleure volonté internationale, en permettant un partenariat de fait avec la société civile, en bâtissant une paix durable, respectueuse de la justice, et en adoptant une approche de la paix et de la sécurité basée sur le leadership féminin. Le leadership féminin doit lui-même être repensé en tenant compte du fait que les femmes en milieu rural constituent 80% de la population féminine.

The Role of the Church in Breaking the Silence against Specific Forms and Patterns of Victimization and Perpetration of Violence in Zimbabwe: From Gukurahundi to Date

Tendaishe Tlou

Abstract

Zimbabwe has perpetrated gross human rights violations, from independence to today. Extra-judicial killings, torture, displacements, enforced disappearances, and detentions, among other human rights violations, have been committed with impunity, and no one has accounted for them. The National Transitional Justice Working Group (NTJWG), among other stakeholders, has raised demands for accountability through transitional justice processes but has not yet fully broken the silence on organized violence and torture (OVT) in the country. Zimbabwe has failed to break the cycle of violence and provide a platform for victims and survivors of *Gukurahundi*: protracted political violence, Operation *Murambatsvina in 2005*, the coup in November 2017, the 1 August 2018 shootings of unarmed civilians in Harare, and most recently, the 14 January 2019 protests. Over the years, women have mostly emerged as victims, yet men also have been affected by this cyclical violence through abductions, extra-judicial killings, and arbitrary arrests on trumped-up charges. Few have spoken out, and in most instances, victims have become perpetrators of violence. It is high time that Zimbabwe, through the National Peace and Reconciliation Commission (NPRC), pays close attention and addresses gender-specific violations over the years by creating safe spaces where boys and men can share their experiences, heal, and lead normal lives in Zimbabwe, otherwise violence and trauma will remain part of the country's present and future.

Introduction

In spite of the overwhelming evidence of gross human rights abuses in Zimbabwe, especially since *Gukurahundi*, which began in 1983 up to today and the accompanying trauma the conflict has imposed on people in Zimbabwe, there remains limited consensus on who are the victims and survivors of these abuses and to what extent the trauma has affected citizens. To date, no one has official records of the victims of past atrocities, notwithstanding the sterling documentation by civil society. Despite having statistics from the Catholic Commission for Justice and Peace in Zimbabwe (CCJPZ) that 20,000 to 30,000 people were killed during *Gukurahundi*,[1] the data still remains unclear and is not conclusive. The *Chihambakwe* Commission of Inquiry report was swept under the rug and was never made available to the nation. Everyone remains in the dark as to what officially transpired. This situation illuminates the fundamental challenges that post-independence African states have in promoting national peace and reconciliation.

In most violent conflict cases, women and children are stereotyped as the ultimate victims, while men are classified as the perpetrators. This has closed off the possibilities of an organic approach to viewing men and women as equal victims in any conflict. This essay seeks to unveil the hidden truth about victims in Zimbabwe and explore what the church in Zimbabwe can do to advance an inclusive approach to national healing, truth recovery, and dealing with trauma. The fact that the National Peace and Reconciliation Commission (NPRC) became operational in January 2018 presents an opportunity for inclusive reconciliation and healing. This can be done by involving ordinary people, particularly Christians, who make up the largest percentage of the population in the country. Most citizens, including church members, were affected in one way or another and therefore were traumatized but have never been given the opportunity to articulate their experiences.

Background of Violence in Zimbabwe

Merely three years into independence, the struggle of the governing party, the Zimbabwe African National Union-Patriotic Front (ZANU-PF), and the Zimbabwe African People's Union (ZAPU) for political hegemony began. Eventually, the power struggles degenerated into the "dissident cleansing" era popularly known as *Gukurahundi,* which lasted from 1983 to 1987.[2] As noted above, the CCJPZ reported that 20,000 to 30,000 people died during

---

1. Catholic Commission for Justice and Peace in Zimbabwe, *Breaking the Silence: Building True Peace – Report on the Disturbances in Matabeleland and the Midlands 1980 to 1988*, (CCJPZ/ LRF: Harare, 1997). Gukurahundi was a military operation by the Government of Zimbabwe from 1983 to 1987 in the southern and central parts of Zimbabwe which left approximately 30,000 people dead and thousands more injured, buried in unmarked graves, among other crimes against humanity.

2. Ibid.

this military operation.[3] This has left a festering and painful wound in the hearts of Zimbabweans, especially among those who directly experienced the atrocities and in the psyches of those who indirectly experienced it. Arguably, both the old and the new generations of the Zimbabwean population are traumatized. The atrocities were halted only by an unprecedented unity government deal between the then ZAPU-PF leader, Joshua Nkomo, and ZANU-PF President and Zimbabwe's Prime Minister, Robert G. Mugabe, which led to PF-ZAPU being assimilated into ZANU-PF.[4] However, the findings of the *Chihambakwe* Commission of Inquiry, instituted in 1988, were not made public even 33 years later.

Despite the overwhelming evidence found in the CCJPZ report, no one has assumed responsibility and accountability[5] for the atrocities because repressive actions by the State were done under the rubric of law, order, and security concerns which "justified" the result. This also meant that no initiatives for trauma healing and counselling were rolled out in Zimbabwe because no one publicly acknowledged these violent incidents. The State acted as if nothing had happened. Even higher rates of torture and its aftereffects were found in studies of the *Gukurahundi* period of the 1980s in Matabeleland. Here, it was found that more than 80 percent of the sample reported torture; the prevalence rate for consequent psychological disorders was 50 percent of all adults over age 18.[6]

After a few years of negative peace and cosmetic stability, the early 1990s were characterized by a pervasive establishment of civil society organizations (CSOs) and the evolution of the Zimbabwe Congress of Trade Unions into a full-fledged political party known as the Movement for Democratic Change (MDC). This was made possible through the convergence of civil society and the church.[7] This development redefined Zimbabwe's socio-political landscape and catapulted the country into a young "democracy." Calls for free and fair elections, the democratization of institutions, constitutionalism,

---

3. Ibid.

4. A. Mutambara, *The One-Party State* (Harare: Mambo Press, 1998).

5. Themba Lesizwe, *Civil Society and Justice in Zimbabwe: Proceedings of a Symposium Held in Johannesburg, 11-13 August 2003* (Pretoria: Themba Lesizwe, 2004).

6. Amani Trust, *Survivors of Organised Violence in Matabeleland: Facilitating an Agenda for Development – Report of the Workshop* (1998).

7. Brian Raftopolus and Alois Mlambo, eds, *Becoming Zimbabwe: A History from the Pre-colonial Period to 2008* (Harare: Weaver Press, 2009).

and good governance increased.[8] The Government of Zimbabwe was faced with a formidable "revolution" of its own kind at a magnitude never experienced before.

In the face of growing resilience and resistance, the State responded by deploying heavily armed police and, army who assaulted, shot, and arrested anyone who stood in their way. This approach hinged on quelling opposition in *Gukurahundi* style. The years between 2000 and 2008 saw the formation of paramilitary State institutions such as the National Youth Service (NYS), which had powers similar to those of the army and police. Young men and women were recruited into the NYS, army and police on an unprecedented scale in the 2000s. Most originated from rural areas where the ruling party retained more support and loyalty to curb dissent by a growing "defiant" urban populace. The State also took advantage of the absence of media in the peripheral areas and whipped rural dwellers into line.

The NYS is the same brigade that was deployed to destroy homes of real and perceived opposition supporters in the urban areas in 2005 under the guise of Operation *Murambatsvina*.[9] Thousands of homes and people's property were destroyed; many people were displaced or forced to return to the rural areas at the beginning of winter in May 2005. Churches and other civil society organizations stepped in to fill the vacuum created by the State by providing temporary shelter, food, clothing, repatriation to rural areas, counselling, and medical assistance, among other things.[10] Fast forward to 2008, the youth brigade also had a hand in the June 2008 election run-off, with the backing of the army and police, which led to the deaths of at least 3,000 people and the displacement of thousands more.[11] This culture of impunity and cyclical violence piled trauma upon trauma on Zimbabwean citizens. Trauma has been reinforced over the years, which also points to the fact that the State is not sincere in addressing the past and promoting trauma healing in the country.

According to Parsons et al.,

> The violence perpetrated in the past few years' most obvious effects are physical, seen in illnesses and injuries, which may be short-lived, but also may lead to long-term disability. However, the most persistent consequences will

---

8. Ibid.

9. Ibid.

10. Ibid.

11. Ibid.

be psychological, and especially if the trauma was deliberately inflicted, as in torture, for example. The most probable long-term consequence of experiencing organized violence and torture is the development of a psychological disorder.[12]

In Zimbabwe, there is the continuous and overt involvement of the army in civilian affairs. In November 2017, the current president, Emmerson D. Mnangagwa, assumed office through a military coup.[13] Eight months later, on 1 August 2018, the military was deployed in the central business district of Harare following protests by alleged opposition supporters due to an alleged deliberate delay in announcing the presidential results by the Zimbabwe Electoral Commission (ZEC). Six unarmed civilians, some of whom were not even part of the demonstrations, were shot and killed in cold blood.[14] The deployment of the army in civilian affairs is worrying. It has since given rise to new questions about transitional justice in Zimbabwe and concerns about whether post-colonial Zimbabwe is committed to implementing substantive national healing and reconciliation processes. I am of the view that due to the unresolved past and recent gross human rights abuses, trauma is manifesting itself in the form of direct violence, and people are increasingly frustrated with draconian laws and the governance systems the government is introducing. Hence, the shutdown protests that led to the death, abduction, and torture of more civilians in January 2019 and the continuous harassment of human rights defenders and opposition leaders up to date.

Due to frustration over the deteriorating socio-economic situation across the country, various labour and political organizations have made efforts to mobilize for protests. However, the State has since prevented that from happening. It is beyond any reasonable doubt that in a nation that is not allowed to vent out its grievances and any dissent met with violence, the citizenry becomes highly traumatized and unsettled. Zimbabwe is a relatively peaceful nation but a highly stressed and divided one that lacks outlets for expressing dissatisfaction and any viable source of relief. As a result, the youth in high-density areas are resorting to dangerous drugs, crime, violence, prostitution and other harmful practices.

---

12. Ross Parsons, Tony Reeler, Jane Fisher and Eugenia Mpande, *Trauma and Mental Health in Zimbabwe* (Harare: Research and Advocacy Unit, 2011).

13. Piers Pigou, "Zimbabwe's Very Peculiar Coup." International Crisis Group, 16 November 2017, at: https://www.crisisgroup.org/africa/southern-africa/zimbabwe/zimbabwes-very-peculiar-coup.

14. *Post-Election Violence Monitoring Report* (Harare: Zimbabwe Human Rights NGO Forum, 2018), https://www.hrforumzim.org/news/2018-post-election-violence-monitoring-report-updated.

In the case of Zimbabwe, the State capitalized on poverty, unemployment, fear, trauma, and suffering to recruit young people into the NYS for the purposes mentioned above. In this case, the youth are victims of the past who end up becoming perpetrators for a violent, corrupt, and manipulative system. After these atrocities, the State has made no effort to support survivors or identify their needs, particularly in the area of truth-recovering and healing from trauma. For example, women and children who were sexually assaulted and violated in a variety of ways during *Gukurahundi* and the political violence have never been contacted and assisted through counselling or any other means. Some are still highly traumatized and feel their experiences as if they had happened yesterday.

Organized violence and torture have been documented in all three of the three most recent decades of Zimbabwe's history. One study showed that one adult in ten over the age of 30 reported having been tortured and was suffering from a clinically significant psychological disorder as a result.[15]

Paying Particular Attention to Gender-Specific Abuses

Research has shown that during periods of violent conflict, young men, boys, girls, and women are easy targets for sodomy and rape. In Zimbabwe, society has many unacknowledged gender-specific violations which occurred specifically from 1983 to the present, but we can even go beyond independence. Violations like the treatment of fellow male "freedom fighters," recruited at a tender age as sex slaves, the mass rape of women and girls as a weapon of war, physical abuse, and discrimination are issues the NPRC, the church, and other stakeholders in Zimbabwe must confront and redress in the next few years as a matter of urgency. These violations have not been given adequate attention, mainly due to arrogance and ignorance. For example, following the January 2019 protests, the government dismissed reports that women were sexually abused by security agents, which compounded the trauma for the women.

The lack of safe spaces to speak about such traumatic experiences or the generic belief that rape is an inevitable consequence of conflict, so you just have to shake it off and move on to avoid humiliating the family and being rejected by society, heightens post-traumatic stress disorder (PTSD) in victims.

15. A.P. Reeler, P. Mbape, J. Matshona, J. Mhetura and E. Hlatywayo, "The Prevalence and Nature of Disorders Due to Torture in Mashonaland Central Province, Zimbabwe," *Torture* 11 (2001), 4–9.

In most instances, people who have been traumatized during conflict are the same people who have become perpetrators, politicians, businesspeople, mothers, fathers, and community leaders. Hence, in my view, the cycle of violence in the country at large and within households is unbreakable and perpetual.

The Role of the Church in the Redress and Restoration of Dignity of Zimbabweans

The Establishment of Effective Support Systems for Survivors

Following the mass genocide in the Matabeleland and Midlands regions and other atrocities towards civilians, the recruitment of boys or girls into militias, and exposure to protracted violence, Zimbabwe still lacks readily available support systems for victims and survivors. Survivors are expected to forgive and forget, despite the trauma they have experienced. In a situation where victim records are not available, most survivors have fallen off the radar and have not received the assistance they deserve. African States have not been vigilant in establishing counselling, rehabilitation, and non-recurrence mechanisms for victims of violence in a post-conflict environment. Worse still, survivors of violence are re-victimized and discriminated against by other community members or leaders with who they regularly associate and are constantly in touch with. The environment is still toxic and unable to assist survivors in recovering from PTSD and other forms of trauma. This is the same community that expects survivors to quickly forget and move on, an approach that is made worse by the fact that there are no readily available counselling services and rehabilitation centres in the communities where sur-vivors reside.

The church in Zimbabwe is strategically positioned as a neutral mediator, which brings politicians, businesspeople, mothers, sons, daughters, and everyone else into one place at the same time. The church can model its intervention based on the scriptures, ensuring that the message appeals to everyone. The church is one of the longest-standing community support systems which can deal with the effects of trauma. Also, most pastors have a strong background in trauma healing and counselling, which can be used to rehabilitate survivors who have been forgotten. People trust men and women of God, as they are popularly referred to in Zimbabwe.

The Creation of Safe Spaces for Victims and Survivors of Past Atrocities in Africa

Africa is still very conservative and not well equipped to provide safe spaces for victims. It is on record that survivors of violent conflict, in many cases, suffer extreme PTSD and are afraid to report violence due to the lack of protection mechanisms and the non-prosecution of perpetrators. In the case of Zimbabwe, survivors are often arrested or ridiculed by the police when they go to report abuse that took place during conflict. Most are accused of inciting or being part of the violence. Meanwhile, it is alleged that the per-petrators of *Gukurahundi* are still in government, and so survivors are afraid to talk openly about their experiences during violent conflicts due to fear of persecution and retaliation by the State.

As someone who worked for the Zimbabwe Council of Churches during the Mugabe era, when talking about *Gukurahundi* was a crime against humanity, I am confident that the church can create mechanisms and a conducive environment that is accommodating, sensitive, and responsive to the needs and suffering of survivors. The church is the only hope for Zimbabwe due to its moral compass and its standing in society which inspires trust and is capable of enabling the country to recover from the memories and experiences of past atrocities through healing, reconciliation, and closure. Survivors should not be re-victimized during rehabilitation and other engagements. In most instances, survivors of violent conflicts still have to wake up and see the perpetrators in the community where they live. Survivors cannot speak about their experiences due to fear of persecution by both supporters of the perpetrator and the perpetrators themselves. Through the church, survivors can be both protected and heard.

Advocacy for Adopting an Inclusive and Sensitive Gender Policy

The push for a National Peace and Reconciliation Commission (NPRC) was difficult and tedious, with the church taking a leading role in mobilizing and amplifying the calls for its adoption. The State, under the administration of former president Robert Mugabe, was very reluctant to engage stakeholders to talk about national peace and reconciliation issues. This was made evident through the president's efforts to conceal evidence and the truth about what exactly happened during *Gukurahundi* and other atrocities after the genocide. Hence, the disappearance of the *Chihambakwe* Commission report to date.

During the forming of the National Constitutional Assembly (NCA) in the early 2000s, the church played a pivotal role in the adoption of a new constitution in 2013, which was more progressive than its predecessor. It is high time that the church also advocates for adopting a national transitional justice policy that puts women, girls, boys, and men at the centre of trauma healing and truth recovery. Capitalizing on the momentum set in the 2000s, the church has since had the mandate to ensure that Zimbabwe has a commission focusing on reconciliation issues derived from the needs and expectations of the people. At a time when the leadership in Zimbabwe disrupted efforts for dialogue, justice, and accountability for past atrocities, the church, through the leadership of the Zimbabwe Council of Churches (ZCC), used "the Zimbabwe We Want" as a blueprint to create the transitional agenda, a people's agenda. This agenda inspired consensus among all stakeholders in Zimbabwe. It took pertinent issues that had been rejected by politicians into urban and rural areas across Zimbabwe, inviting the people to speak and express their views on transitional justice, truth, and healing processes.

Advocacy around such issues is critical in elevating the people's agenda above political expediency and setting an agenda for the government to establish a national historical dialogue platform that articulates the views of the masses on truth and trauma healing.

Including the National Peace and Reconciliation Commission in the New Constitution

On 22 May 2013, then president Robert Mugabe signed into law the new Constitution of Zimbabwe, following a constitutional reform process dating back to 1999.[16] One of the key features of this constitution is chapter 12, which establishes five independent commissions supporting democracy.[17] One of the independent commissions is the National Peace and Reconciliation Commission (NPRC), which has the duty to ensure post-conflict justice, healing, and reconciliation. This commission represents the efforts of many organizations, including churches, victim groups, non-governmental organizations (NGOs), and international organizations, which have been clamouring for a peace commission to help Zimbabwean society come to terms with its violent past.

____

16. This section is well articulated in NTJWG, *A Guide to Understanding the National Peace and Reconciliation Commission in Zimbabwe,* 2nd ed. (Harare: National Transitional Justice Working Group Zimbabwe, 2018), https://ntjwg.uwazi.io/en/document/70r8ui4hl1k.

17. Ibid.

It represents the hopes of many victims and survivors of past human rights violations that truth, justice, and healing may see the light of the day. The successes and failures of the NPRC remain to be seen, but what is clear is that an important conversation has already started. It took the Government of Zimbabwe five years to operationalize the commission, implying that the commission is behind schedule in implementing its mandate, which is disturbing. The Zimbabwe Human Rights Forum published another document focusing on how far back the commission should go in addressing national peace and reconciliation issues.

Adoption of the NPRC Act and Operationalization of the National Peace and Reconciliation Commission

From 2016, the Parliament of Zimbabwe debated the law to enable the NPRC to carry out its work. This followed a second round of consultations that were done after the people of Zimbabwe and the civil society, under the banner of the Forum and others, vehemently rejected the first draft as being inadequate in the context of the country. On 5 January 2018, the Government of Zimbabwe gazetted the *NPRC Act*, fully operationalizing the commission.[18] The law establishes and regulates the NPRC.

Identifying and Addressing Gaps in the Act

Regarding gender, section (9) (i) of the Act obliges the commission to establish a Gender Unit, which infuses gender as a cross-cutting issue in all its work. However, taking into consideration the theme of the 2018 Institute for African Transitional Justice programme, the Act is inadequate to specifically address the gender-specific harms against men and boys because it assumes the reductionist approach of classifying women and girls as the prime victims. The opposite sex is totally left out of the picture. The Act is relatively silent on the experiences of women, boys, and men with regards to mental health issues; thus, this can be put on the agenda as an advocacy point of entry to influence the NPRC to change its perspective. The reconciliation process must be aware of the gendered aspects of conflict transformation, the gender dynamics of men and women, and the documentation and memorialization of such experiences.[19]

---

18. Ibid.

19. Dzikamai Bere, "How to Kill a Peace Commission at Birth," The Standard, 19 March 2017, https://www.thestandard.co.zw/2017/03/19/kill-peace-commission-birth.

This discourse goes beyond crimes against women: it should bring in the structural and cultural aspects that shape and make possible such violations. This should include identifying establishing structures that specifically address mental health issues and trauma. The rates of suicide and mental health problems in Africa are too high, particularly in countries such as Zimbabwe, South Sudan, and South Africa, which were or still are going through protracted conflict.

According to a World Health Organization report on prevalence estimates of mental health disorders in conflict and post-conflict settings, the effect of conflict on people's mental health is higher than what previous estimates indicated. The report highlights that about one in five people in post-conflict settings have depression, anxiety disorder, PTSD, bipolar disorder, or schizophrenia.[20] If the *NPRC Act* remains silent on mental health issues, the situation could deteriorate further, to the detriment of psycho-social sanity in the country and the continent as a whole. Mental health and psycho-social support should be readily available to people in both conflict and post-conflict situations. Institutions responsible for national peace and reconciliation processes should make this a priority. If it is neglected, trauma might be expressed in destructive ways, such as physical or direct violence.

The case of South Africa is appealing. According to the Dutch Minister of Foreign Trade and Development Co-operation, "if we want to truly help a country with reconstruction, we shouldn't just rebuild the bombed bridges. We should also help people repair their broken souls."[21] This is easier said than done; it entails political will from all stakeholders: the NPRC, civil society organizations, and up to the highest office in the land, the presidency. Transitional justice is a relatively new phenomenon in Africa. Research should be done, and resources should be made available, as mental health issues are overt and people need to be motivated and supported to share their experiences.

---

20. Fiona Charlson, Mark van Ommeren, Abraham Flaxman, Joseph Cornette, Harvey Whiteford and Shekhar Saxena, "New WHO Prevalence Estimates of Mental Disorders in Conflict Settings: A Systematic Review and Meta-Analysis," The Lancet 394: 10194 (2019), https://www.thelancet.com/journals/lancet/article/PIIS0140-6736(19)30934-1/fulltext.

21. Sigrid Kaag, "War's Trauma Endures Long after the Last Shot Is Fired – Broken Souls Need Rebuilding," *The Guardian*, 30 June 2019, https://www.theguardian.com/society/2019/jun/30/wars-trauma-endures-long-after-the-last-shot-is-fired-broken-souls-need-rebuilding.

The church can work with the commission and Parliament to integrate mental health issues in the Act. Most importantly, the Act can empower the commission, the church, and other stakeholders to work together to train its workforce and make mental health services widely available. This can be done by disseminating mental health services to the grassroots by developing skills for practitioners to make it an integral part of their intervention strategies. Mental health should be made a cross-cutting issue to bridge the mental health services gap.

It is important that the church, working with other stakeholders, integrates mental health and psycho-social support in all its transitional justice interventions. The church is rich in pastors who are trained in counselling as their primary function to assist couples, women, men, children, and youth. Therefore, it is commendable for the church to frame and develop transitional justice initiatives which responds to the needs of the people with whom they interact frequently. Transitional justice works when the process is inclusive, interactive, and consultative. In the process of providing counselling services to survivors, the church can supply relevant information to official transitional justice processes such as the NPRC so that mental health issues are incorporated into existing transitional justice structures.

The Role of the Church in Enabling Truth-seeking and Truth-telling (Promotion of Truth)

Truth-seeking

The promotion of truth is one of the most important pillars in transitional justice processes. It can be divided into two components: truth-seeking and truth-telling. Truth-seeking can be described as a mission to discover, clarify, and formally acknowledge past abuses in search of the truth. It can be done in many ways. It enables people to do what is necessary to build and sustain democracy, examine the crimes of the past, learn about the myths and the facts of the violations, understand what lies underneath, and come to terms with it. Truth-seeking can be based on initiatives of local organizations. Examples include information gathering on violations and human rights abuses by (human rights) NGOs or religious organizations or by academic institutions when the government does not take the lead in bringing accountability to the country's dark past.

When talking about transitional justice mechanisms, truth-seeking is often mentioned in the same breath as truth-telling.

Truth-telling

When testifying in court, the witness promises, by swearing or affirming, that "the evidence that I shall give shall be the truth, the whole truth and nothing but the truth." The truth has the ability to free and unburden a person. If it is done effectively, truth-telling can be a mechanism for healing from trauma.

People generally define the concept of truth as an objective and unchangeable fact, but at the same time, many admit that truth depends on the various perspectives of individuals, which is relative. In transitional justice, the church should create safe spaces where witnesses, victims and survivors of past atrocities can narrate their experiences without fear, which will enable healing, forgiveness and sustainable peace.

If it is made difficult for people to talk about their experiences in the open, victims tend to isolate themselves in their community and talk about their experiences only in their inner circles. This enhances the feelings of anger and hatred against the "others" or the real or perceived perpetrator, which is likely to result in violence rather than reconciliation. This is the case in Zimbabwe, specifically in the context of *Gukurahundi*, Operation *Murambatsvina*, politically motivated violence, and Operation *Hakudzokwe*. A lot has happened in Zimbabwe, yet no adequate spaces have been created for people to talk about their experiences. This is the missing link that can enable the restoration of mental wellbeing in the country.

Conclusion

Zimbabwe is a country that has undergone wave after wave of atrocities and violent conflict. Yet not enough platforms have been created for people to speak and share their experiences. It is against this background that the short- and long-term effects of violence on the masses have been traumatic. Given that, according to a recent study, at least 80 percent of Zimbabweans are Christians who attend at least one church service a week, the church can play a pivotal role in resolving mental health issues in the country. The church can use its access to the masses, its reach, its capacity, and its skills to push for a mental health agenda in Zimbabwe. This can be done through specialized programmes, such as counselling, and basic sessions such as dialogue, truth-seeking, and truth-telling. Mental health issues caused by conflict in the country should be taken seriously – something that is long overdue in Zimbabwe.

12

Healing the Traumatized as a New-alternative Mission Field:
The Experience of the Ethiopian Evangelical Church Mekane Yesus
among the Oromo-Gumuz Communities in Western Ethiopia

Moti Daba Fufa

Abstract

Ethiopia is an ancient and multicultural country which has experienced minimal tensions. And yet, the Oromo and Gumuz communities are among the most conflicted regions in Ethiopia due to border conflicts. The purpose of this essay is to show the experience of the Ethiopian Evangelical Church Mekane Yesus in healing trauma resulting from the ethnic conflict between these two communities. In addition, the essay argues that healing trauma through truth and strengthening cooperation with responsible stakeholders in the 21st century is a crucial issue that requires intervention by contemporary churches.

Introduction

The purpose of this essay is to bring to light the amazing experience of the Ethiopian Evangelical Church Mekane Yesus (EECMY) in mediating healing of traumatic pain resulting from ethnic conflict between the Oromo and Gumuz communities in Western Ethiopia in recent decades. The EECMY is the largest and fastest-growing church in the Lutheran communion of churches. It is also a member of the World Council of Churches and the All Africa Conference of Churches. The essay describes several peace initiatives and activities that have taken place to heal broken relationships and mediate this conflict through the EECMY Peace Office and other bodies, such as local communities, regional governments, and international organizations.

This essay argues that healing the experience of trauma in the 21st century is a crucial issue that requires interventions by today's churches, such as the EECMY. This can be accomplished by fostering an environment for healing the wounds through truth-telling and strengthening cooperation between local communities and among regional governments in partnership with responsible stakeholders. Trauma causes a person or community to experience a series of repeated disturbances or to be deeply wounded. This in turn creates sensitivity to the fear that one is in an unsafe environment. It continuously affects one's memory as well as one's relationship to God, self, and community. Therefore, healing trauma may be a new-alternative mission field for today's churches. In this way, the EECMY promotes a worthwhile missional approach to bring comfort, hope, and life to a broken relationship among communities through meeting the whole aspects of their human needs, such as spiritual, social, emotional, psychological, and physical.

The Oromo–Gumuz case is the most astounding and relevant case of the healing of trauma; it was initiated by the EECMY as a project from 2012 to 2017 to reconcile these communities and heal their wounds. As a result, hundreds of congregations participated in this pilgrimage and witnessed their fellowship, celebrating life together and engaging in transformative action for a peaceful and healthy society.

This essay begins with a brief historical development of how the cause of the conflict has led to the two community congregations being separated into two groups, then explores different approaches used in healing trauma and assesses the impacts of the approaches. Finally, the author invites readers to further develop a methodology for pastoral healing responses for those who are serving people who have had traumatic experiences. In addition, the essay is a call to churches to be on the side of the oppressed to comfort them, listen to their stories, pray together, and give hope in the everyday lives of many people who have deep-rooted wounds.

Healing Trauma through Truth as the Main Strategy of the New-alternative Mission Field for the Church

> Again I saw all the oppressions that are practised under the sun. Look, the tears of the oppressed—with no one to comfort them! On the side of their oppressors there was power—with no one to comfort them. (Eccles. 4:1, NRSV)

The Greek word for "trauma," τραυμα, has an equivalent meaning: "injury" or "wound."[1] Trauma is an extremely disturbing experience related to a person or community dealing with a series of repeated deep wounds. Sigmund Freud defined trauma as "any excitation that comes from outside that is influential and powerful enough to break through the protective shield."[2] In general, trauma can be initiated either internally with the

---

1. "Trauma," Merriam-Webster's Dictionary, at: https://www.merriam-webster.com/dictionary/trauma
2. Sigmund Freud, *Beyond the Pleasure Principle*, vol. 18 (London: Hogarth, 1920), 7–64, at 32.

individual within a psychic struggle or externally in response to violence, disasters, or catastrophic situations. Explicitly, community trauma is violence which happened intentionally or suddenly in the midst of the community. The experience makes them fearful, terrified, feeling that they are in an unsafe environment. It is mainly related to helplessness; it leads to emotional scars and leaves people feeling physically vulnerable. It can induce cognitive deterioration or may lead to revenge and violence.

According to Werner Bohleber, who studied trauma in both individuals and the broader community, "The excessive distractions and extreme experiences that people underwent and suffered in this century turned trauma into its hallmark."[3] Bohleber notes that there was a growing need for investigation and understanding—not only in terms of treatment but also in the other human sciences. However, I have observed that the problem goes beyond the human sciences. I argue that only trauma which is healed through genuine truth and reconciliation can be a new-alternative mission field for today's church. This new-alternative mission field addresses the whole person by responding to the deep wounds and traumatic experiences on an individual or community level for several years.

Traditionally, in the context of Ethiopia, the responsibility for reconciliation between two or more communities belongs to the government or, more specifically, to the respective regional state figures. Religious leaders are usually invited for ceremonial blessings with respected elders. This may be because of the separation between church and state. Furthermore, the holistic ministry includes the soul, the mind, the social, and the physical needs of people. Mission work, however, has traditionally been mostly focused on the salvation of the soul. On the other hand, there is an alternative approach to reconciliation between communities which includes religious leaders as forerunners of reconciliation and healing trauma. This approach can foster healing the wounds through truth-telling and strengthening cooperation with religious organizations in partnership with responsible stakeholders. Healing trauma in such a way is a new-alternative mission field for the EECMY that promotes a worthy missional approach to bring comfort, hope, and life to a broken relationship among communities through meeting spiritual, emotional, psychological, and physical needs.

---

3. Werner Bohleber, "Remembrance, Trauma and Collective Memory: The Battle for Memory in Psychoanalysis," *International Journal of Psychoanalysis* 38 (2007), 329–52.

First, traumatic experience abuses and violates the whole person, which includes their physical body, spiritual life, beliefs, feelings, and even knowledge. It affects the relationship between God, self, and communities that continues in other life memories. The church must recognize this traumatic experience, which affects the emotional, spiritual, and physical. This new-alternative mission field may create an opportunity for the church to tackle unjust systems that deny the equality of human beings and the rights of all. Healing traumatic memories requires an urgent response: we must bring solutions and answers to unprecedented traumatic consequences that extend from generation to generation.

Second, human beings have a mutual vertical and horizontal relationship with God and self, other human beings, and ecology, respectively, which in cases of trauma has been broken through mistrust and violence. Needless to say, in such cases it is hard to maintain the relationship between the affected individuals and the community. The church must recognize this and boldly speak about the true potential experience of trauma: being traumatized means being trapped in the cycle of violence, losing relationships, and breaking the basic trust of individuals or a community. This may also lead to the distortion of God's creation.

Third, churches must reflect a pilgrimage of justice and peace as a global church during a conflict situation that violates human dignity, including violence emanating from racism, gender-based violence, and displacement.[4] Justice and peace are the two major essentials for a life of unity and dignity within the church and in our relationship to the community. Biblically informed justice and peace are pilgrimages into God's will for human beings and for the whole of creation. In many conflicts, people victimize and oppress human dignity and the will of God; this calls for healing the broken relationship. This healing service of the oppressed is based on respect for a human being wonderfully made in God's image, without any segregation in terms of caste, race, ethnicity, skin colour, social status, gender, and so on. These classifications sometimes create unjust systems that deny the equality of human beings and the rights of all. However, the local or global church prophetically speaks strongly the scriptural passage which reveals that humans are created in God's own self-actualization through humankind (Gen. 1:27).

---

4. World Council of Churches, "Invitation to the Pilgrimage of Justice and Peace," 2018, https://www.oikoumene.org/en/resources/documents/central-committee/geneva-2014/an-invitation-to-the-pilgrimage-of-justice-and-peace.

In general, traumatized memories need to be recovered through authentic and genuine deep healing of wounds. This process embraces true reconciliation that heals and transforms the relationship to produce transformative action. Therefore, healing the traumatized relationship is a holistic ministry that addresses the physical, intellectual, emotional, and spiritual life. This new-alternative mission field can heal the severely damaged relationship, mending broken hearts and showing our love to one another by fulfilling the commandments of Jesus Christ.

The church must demonstrate its active participation in trauma healing as a new-alternative mission in a healthy way and speak the truth about the potential experience of trauma in relation to ethnic conflict. This process invites contemporaries, such as the EECMY church, to heal traumatic experiences and conflicts as a new-alternative mission field among individuals, families, communities, border conflicts, countries, and even continents.

The Cause, Development, and Impacts of the Conflict in the Oromo–Gumuz Community

"The Africa We Want" – namely, Agenda 2063 – is a framework document for transforming Africa into a peaceful and secure continent, with an ambitious deadline in which all guns will be silent by the year 2020.[5] The Horn of Africa has the distinctive feature of being the most intensely conflicted region in Africa. Conflicts are rooted in power struggles, political instability, and border and ethnic conflicts. Western Ethiopia was one of the conflict-prone zones because of Oromo–Gumuz, which was greatly affected including through the loss of many lives and destroyed properties. To further understand the present conflict, we need to consider the historical background.

Oromo and Gumuz: Historical Background

The Oromo and Gumuz communities have had a long history in Ethiopia. These communities shared borders, economies, and certain cultures; some people from these communities even intermarried. On the other hand, the communities have also experienced unpleasant relationships. The major cause of the conflict was a struggle over resource competition and power-sharing

---

5. African Union Commission, Agenda 2063: The Africa We Want, 2015, https://au.int/sites/default/files/documents/33126-doc-01_background_note.pdf.

due to spontaneous large-scale migration from other regions.[6] As a result, the Gumuz community claims, the central government supports the community when it comes to land grabbing, cultural clashes, forced assimilation, and other forms of discrimination. These problems are considered a watershed for resource competition, power sharing, and ethnic identity conflicts. The Gumuz community claimed to restore the land they thought was unjustly taken away from their forefathers by the Oromo community leaders. As for the Oromo, the community did not and still does not accept this justification by Gumuz; Oromo claims that the territorial dimensions of Oromia are wider than what was established by the current government.

The conflict has affected Christian fellowship as one body in Jesus Christ for both communities. Emmanuel Abraham, the emeritus president of the EECMY, asserted in his book *Reminiscences of My Life* that the Oromo–Gumuz communities had a long-standing enmity and mutual suspicion.[7] He added that the two communities did not accept each other, which has affected the expansion of the gospel. This eruption might have led to several causes of the conflict between the two communities, even among EECMY believers.

Incidents of violent conflict between Oromo and Gumuz began in 1993. However, the major incident took place on 28 September 1994. After 1994, there were repeated eruptions of violence mainly due to aggravating conflict for territorial insecurity and border conflict.

The Internal Displacement Monitoring Center (IDMC) reported in 2009 that growing tensions between the two communities resulted in killings and woundings in 2008.[8] IDMC added that the conflict stemmed from the death of hundreds; also, clashes among ethnic groups led to the displacement of tens of thousands of persons. This resulted in strong fighting breaking out between the two groups. During the conflict, hundreds of people died, and many families were displaced, including women, children, and the elderly. EECMY congregations from both sides were highly affected. The conflict also occurred between the two communities in the Kamashi and Eastern Wollega zones, within the EECMY Central Synod working area, which affected the

---

6. "Ethiopia: Situation of the Shinasha Ethnic Group, Including Treatment by the Majority Population and Authorities (2012–July 2014)," UNHCR, Refworld, at: https://www.refworld.org/docid/54bf5e6d4.html.

7. Emmanuel Abraham, *Reminiscences of My Life* (Trenton: Red Sea Press, 1995), 267.

8. Internal Displacement Monitoring Centre and Norwegian Refugee Council, *Ethiopia: Human Rights Violations and Conflicts Continue to Cause Displacement*, 3 September 2009, https://www.refworld.org/pdfid/4aa0e1472.pdf.

relationship of some congregations.

The conflict was reported by the Central Synod and, at the same time, the EECMY Peace Office was asked to assess it. The EECMY Peace Office did a preliminary assessment of the situation and its challenges, with financial support from the Evangelical Lutheran Free Church of Norway / Norwegian Missions in Development. The EECMY took this opportunity to assess as a project, from 2012 to 2017, reconciling and healing the deep wounds of the two communities.

The conflict between the two communities which broke out in 2008 penetrated different congregations and created fear and mistrust among Oromo and Gumuz believers and ministers within one church where these two peoples worship together. For instance, Mekane Yesus congregations in Horewata, Gumuz, stopped communicating with Oromo Mekane Yesus congregations. Evangelists and ministers stopped visiting each other. It was also impossible to organize worship conferences together.

The outcome of this conflict was traumatic experiences, deep wounds, insecurity, injustice, suffering, displacement, dislocation, burning of churches, the loss of many lives, and the destruction of property. During the conflict, there was an extreme act in which a group of choir members were burned alive while practising songs in the congregation. The experience of this conflict and violence brought disorder to communities, breaking down cultural values, religious teachings, ethical conduct, and traditional reconciliation in both communities, which disrupted both groups.

On both sides, the traumatic experience brought destruction and breakup as a community. Many husbands were tempted to join armed rebel groups and leave their families behind. Elderly people, women, and young girls faced many exceptional pressures, including gender-based violence and rape, that may have contributed to sexually transmitted diseases. Children who survived the conflict failed to see any future hope and move beyond these painful memories. The experience of trauma is not always visible on the outside of the body. As the writer of Proverbs (18:14) asks, "The human spirit will endure sickness; but a broken spirit—who can bear?" Such trauma and deep wounds resulted in bitter distress, broken-heartedness, painful memories, and erratic relationships toward others.

The Role of the EECMY Peace Office in Conflict Resolution and Trauma Healing, and Impacts of the Approach

The EECMY is known by its motto, which is addressing the holistic ministry on the soil of Ethiopia. Furthermore, the church strives to work for justice and peace; it established an office in 1998 with the aim of "making the prophetic voice of the church heard and equipping the members of the church for peace building."[9] Therefore, the church also offers peace education, advocacy, conflict management, and interreligious cooperation by integrating evangelism and development programs.

The EECMY actively participates in peace building in Ethiopia. The church also has experience resolving its own internal conflicts, which arose from a rift in the church that involved more than 12 years of painful situations. This conflict was resolved within the church through the mediation of church leaders; the wounds were healed, and leaders have been celebrating life together since 2012. Another case worth mentioning is a mediating role by the EECMY that happened among Muslims and evangelical Christians in Jimma in 2011. This conflict resulted in the suffering of thousands of people and destroyed more than 60 churches. The EECMY has also successfully accomplished this mission in collaboration with the Inter-religious Council of Ethiopia, with local government and international partners.

Based on the above and other experiences, the church took initiatives to reconcile and build peace among the Oromo and Gumuz communities by calling on congregations from the conflict area and holding the central synod in 2012. Before the church's involvement, different types of trauma healing were begun among Oromo and Gumuz communities by traditional elders, local security offices, and others, but these were not successful until the EECMY started its own initiatives. Some of the reasons for the lack of success early on were a shortage of skilled and experienced human resources; the project office location being far from the conflict zone; a high level of bureaucratic procedures of the local government; and a lack of local sectors, such as religious organizations, elders, and other stakeholders. The EECMY approaches were unique in several ways, including having skilled and experienced people and gathering different stakeholders to create a peaceful environment between the Oromo and Gumuz communities.

---

9. "Ethiopian Evangelical Church Mekane Yesus," World Council of Churches, https://www.oikoumene.org/member-churches/ethiopian-evangelical-church-mekane-yesus-eecmy.

The intervention was a five-year Peace Project that was implemented between 2012 and 2017.[10] During this phase of intervention, the conflict situation was assessed, trainers were trained, and, based on the findings of the assessment, peace and reconciliation conferences were organized and carried out in two places. Peace committees were established whose membership included all the districts involved in the conflict.

Over the five years, the church used several training approaches to heal the wounds of the two communities. The EECMY Peace Office ran major project activities, such as training on trauma healing, peaceful coexistence for peasant associations, and conflict prevention. As well, it offered a training of trainers program designed for churches and local governments on domestic violence and related courses for those who have not had formal education in training.

The church organized sports activities for young boys and girls as well as art programs on gender-based violence. Besides this, the church organized frequent conferences, such as a peace-related activity, including a peace walk and a peace plant that are still successful and continue to have an impact in other schools. The church also established peace clubs in the school and joint peace committees. In addition, the church published and produced educational modules on existing Ethiopian laws and Bible education with respect to domestic violence, including reading materials for peace clubs.

Another healing approach was a peace-building seminar: it included reading aloud the agreed-upon points of the participants after a thorough discussion on the role of all stakeholders to bring back peace and a goodwill relationship into the two communities which were disturbed by the conflict.[11] In this peace seminar, more than 70 participants attended from the different districts, along with peace club leaders, faith-based leaders, community elders, women, and youth of the two communities. Although the seminar was to be concluded after the presentation of the group discussion and the plenary session, community elders and religious leaders asked for a symbolic reconciliation between the two communities to happen right in the seminar hall. The participants agreed.

---

10. Eyob Yisak, *Narrative Report of the Oromo-Gumuz Communities Peace Project, January 2012–April 2017*, Ethiopian Evangelical Church Mekane Yesus Peace Office.

11. Eyob Yisak, *Mission Report on Oromo-Gumuz Peace Project, Peace Seminar* with School Peace Clubs and Joint Peace Committee Members at Soghe, 24 December 2013, Ethiopian Evangelical Church Mekane Yesus Peace Office.

The EECMY Peace Office also set up information centres in Oromo and Gumuz. These were included in the Oromo-Gumuz Peace Project document as one of the major activities in 2013. To accomplish this idea, the EECMY Peace Office invited government officials of the two regional states, the zonal administration, and security bureaus for a consultation meeting on the paper for a sense of sustainable peace in the regions. Local government bodies, in particular administrative and security offices, should provide offices and human resources such as a key person who will be directly responsible for the information centres. The local government should also submit quarterly reports to the respective church synods. This helped the office to carry out the process with clear and adequate information to do a proper analysis of conflict situations. Without a proper analysis, it is impossible to intervene for successful conflict resolution.

Another peace-building strategy was friendly sports matches between the communities. The sports activities by the young boys and girls had a positive impact on the communities. Based on Eyob Yisak's mid-term report to the church leaders:

> In my assessment and from the reports from local government bodies and the society, the festival has revived the fellowship between the youths of the two communities. It had brought a great impact reducing the tension between the two people. At this time, the second round sport for the peace festival is being organized in Harolimu Wereda. The community is expecting the festival with great joy and they have shown their appreciation by contributing money for the construction of the playground although it was not requested by Peace Office.[12]

The trauma healing process was successful, which brought about a transformative and positive change in the communities; they have been able to pass on the healing they received to their community. In particular, participants who attended the Peaceful Coexistence for Peasant Associations and conflict prevention training are active in their communities with other stakeholders to this day. Today, religious leaders from different religions have participated and have come to an understanding of working together to end the conflict situations. At the same time, officials from both local government and synod offices, including women, have shared their experience through the support of the EECMY Peace Office. Officials report from the different districts what is happening in their area and how they handle issues related to domestic and gender-based violence.

---

12. Yisak, *Narrative Report of the Oromo-Gumuz Peace Project.*

According to the reports given by the local government bodies (zone and district officials) after the project was implemented, tensions between the two peoples in the affected areas has been reduced, cooperation between joint peace committees has improved, and common marketplaces have been revived, bringing the two groups to negotiate together.[13] Government officials and church leaders in the area have developed conflict resolution skills.

According to the United Nations Office for the Coordination of Humanitarian Affairs, in 2019, Ayantu Desta allowed more than 3,000 internally displaced persons to fetch water from her tap and covered high water bills for more than six months.[14] Ayantu said, "I am a mother. I cannot afford to neglect my duty to help children in difficult circumstances." Aynatu is indeed an exemplary woman: she carried the burden of her regular job, caring for her family, and at the same time assisting internally displaced persons for more than six months in Nedjo Town.

Conclusion and Lessons Learned

Today more than ever, Christians come together to engage in promoting peace and justice in a fragmented world as an alternative mission field. Local congregations and leaders have a responsibility to take a side in favour of speaking the truth. They must heal broken relationships that are due to injustice in light of the word of God when unjust rulers violate human dignity through a corrupt system. This makes the church more proactive, more visible in the midst of society and in her mission responsibility. This prophetic voice addresses the whole person.

Further, this understanding helps the church and the work of congregations to engage with and sustain their commission of being an agent for a genuine transformative change of society, with the help of the Holy Spirit, by reaching out with and extending the love of Christ. In this way, the church continues to be a source of hope, comfort, and life when injustice and violence appear.

In community reconciliation and trauma-healing processes, the participation of natural leaders and educated women is crucial and significant.

---

13. For example, the Gumuz people, who had avoided going to the Sughe market (a common market found in Harolimu District), have started going there again. Eyob Yisak, Oromo-Gumuz Peace Project, *Mid-term Narrative Report from January 2012–April 2014*, Ethiopian Evangelical Church Mekane Yesus Peace Office.

14. "Ethiopia Humanitarian Bulletin Issue #13," ReliefWeb bulletin, 29 July–11 August 2019, https://reliefweb.int/report/ethiopia/ethiopia-humanitarian-bulletin-issue-13-29-july-11-august-2019.

Empowering women with the tools of trauma-healing and post-conflict peace-building enables them to work with others for the sustainability of peace.

It takes time for healing approaches and the impact of these approaches to help people and societies recover fully from harsh experiences. The Oromo–Gumuz peace project turned into a process that has brought a great opportunity for the two peoples to sit together to find solutions to their problems and engage in transformative actions. Through the local congregations of the EECMY in Oromo and Gumuz, communities continue to address the healing approaches. They demonstrate concrete solidarity with all human dignity as they face their own past and work for transformative action in relation to their own people. The healing of trauma is not an event we can do at the project level; rather, it is a process that takes time to bring about reconciliation, to heal the wounds, and to engage in positive action toward a society of peace and wellbeing.

CONTRIBUTORS

Adera, Godfrey Owino. Kenya. Minister in the Anglican Church in Kenya. He graduated with a first-class honours in Bachelors of Divinity from St. Paul's University in 2017, Masters of Theology from the Global Institute of Theology - Yonsei university in Korea.

Bitchatou, Agnim Valery. Togo. Il est titulaire d'une licence en sociologie de la santé et du développement. Chrétien catholique engagé, il est militant des droits de l'Homme et activiste LGBT au Togo. Avec plusieurs casquettes, je dirige un réseau d'association identitaire dénommé réseau Cupidon.

Chitambo, Mberikokwazvo Ian. Zimbabwe. A Catholic Brother training for the priesthood with the congregation of the Missionary Oblates of Mary Immaculate. He graduated with a Bachelor of Arts Degree in Philosophy (Cum Laude) and Bachelor of Theology Degree from St Joseph's Theological Institute in South Africa. In his pastoral ministry, Mberikwazvo has worked in countries such as Cameroon, Botswana, Lesotho and Zambia, characterizing the missionary aspect of his vocation.

Fufa, Moti Daba. Ethiopia. Evangelical Church Mekane Yesus (EECMY). Coordinator of the "Urban Mission and Youth Development" Department at EECMY - Addis Ababa Synod.

Kwizera, Emmanuel. Rwanda. Minister in the Presbyterian Church of Rwanda. Bachelor's degree in Protestant Theology from the Protestant Institute of Arts and Social Sciences (PIASS). Charge of Theological Education by Extension (TEE) in the Center of Training and Documentation (CFD) of the Presbyterian Church of Rwanda (EPR) 2015-2019.

Makoetje, Malebona. Lesotho. Member of the Lesotho Evangelical Church in Southern Africa, Mankoaneng LECSA. Part of the youth league and Sunday school teacher.

Mkandawire, Damon. Zambia. Minister of word and sacraments in the United Church of Zambia, where he serves as Hospital Administrator for the United Church of Zambia Mbereshi Mission Hospital. He is also an environmentalist, an upcoming young theologian, and a gender justice activist. He spent years as an Environmental Officer at the Konkola Copper Mines, one of Africa's largest producers of copper, and continues to work towards national and international environmental justice.

Mongo-Bouya, Grâce Pericles. Democratic Republic of Congo. Église Évangélique du Congo (EEC), Délégué de la jeunesse de l'EEC à la CETA, Secrétaire Paroissial de la jeunesse, membre du Conseil Consultatif de la Jeunesse en République du Congo, né le 06 Décembre 1993 à Brazzaville en République du Congo, Célibataire, Économiste.

Niyonsaba, Francoise. Rwanda. Reverend in the Presbyterian Church of Rwanda. Currently, she is Internship Pastor. Student of Master of Theology in Community Care and Development at the Protestant University of Rwanda.

Nyembo, Elie Sango. The Democratic Republic of Congo. A Roman Catholic priest of the Missionaries of Africa (White Fathers), working in a Parish of the Diocese of Tete, Mozambique. Worked in Zambia 2012-2014. From 2015-2018 theological studies at St Joseph's Theological Institute (CEDARA) in South Africa and was ordained priest in December 2018 in Lubumbashi.

Ogidis, Moses Iliya. Nigeria. Pastor at Evangelical Church Winning All (ECWA). Currently: PhD Student at St. Paul's University, Limuru, Kenya. Specialization: New Testament. He has B.A. in Religious Studies/ Theology from the University of Ibadan (2007-2011) and M.A in Theology from ECWA Theological Seminary, Igbaja (2011-2012).

Phiri, Isabel Apawo PhD, Prof Malawi/Switzerland. Presbyterian; Deputy General Secretary for Public Witness and Diakonia of the World Council of Churches; Honorary Professor of the School of Religion, Philosophy and Classics at the University of KwaZulu Natal; Former General Coordinator of the Circle of Concerned African Women Theologians.

Shava, Collins Kudakwashe. Zimbabwe/Kenya. Executive Secretary, Youth at All Africa Conference of Churches (AACC-CETA). He is a holder of a Masters in Public Policy and Governance from Africa University (Zimbabwe). He is a former program assistant for economic justice & youth empowerment at the Zimbabwe Council of Churches (ZCC). He is also a researcher in climate change and environmental issues.

Tlou, Tendaishe. Zimbabwe. A freelance researcher and advocacy practitioner specializing in human rights, peace and transitional justice issues. He holds a BSc (Hons) Degree in Peace and Governance from Bindura University (Zimbabwe) and a Masters in Human Rights, Peace and Development from Africa University (Zimbabwe). Worked for the Alliance for Historical Dialogue and Accountability (AHDA): October 2020 to May 2021. Fellow at the Institute for the Study of Human Rights, Columbia University.

WCC Publications 2018-2021

A comprehensive list of WCC Publications can be found on the Resources section of https://www.oikoumene.org

Donald Norwood, *Pilgrimage of Faith: The Journey of the WCC,* 2018, ISBN: 978-2-8254-1710-2

Carlos Sentado and Manuel Quintero Perez, *A Legacy of Passionate Ecumenism,* 2018, ISBN: 978-2-8254-1711-9

Susan Durber and Fernando Enns (Eds.), *Walking Together: Reflections on the Ecumenical Pilgrimage of Justice and Peace,* 2018, ISBN: 978-2-8254-1712-6

J. Michael West and Gunnar Mägi (Eds.), *Your Word Is Truth: The Bible in Ten Christian Traditions,* 2018, ISBN: 978-2-8254-1714-0

J. Michael West and Gunnar Mägi (Eds.), *Your Word Is Truth: The Bible in Ten Christian Traditions,* eBook edition, 2018, ISBN: 978-2-8254-1715-7

Treatment Adherence and Faith Healing in the Context of HIV and AIDS in Africa (EHAIA), 2018, ISBN: 978-2-8254-1716-4

Treatment Adherence and Faith Healing in the Context of HIV and AIDS in Africa (EHAIA), Kiswahili edition, 2018, ISBN: 978-2-8254-1717-1

Treatment Adherence and Faith Healing in the Context of HIV and AIDS in Africa (EHAIA), French, 2018, ISBN: 978-2-8254-1718-8

Positive Masculinities and Femininities: Handbook for Adolescents and Young People in Faith Communities in Nigeria, English edition, 2018, ISBN: 978-2-8254-1719-5

Translating the Word, Transforming the World: An Ecumenical Reader, 2018 ISBN: 978-2-8254-1712-6

Amélé Adamavi-Aho Ekué, Pamela D. Couture, and Samuel George (Eds.), *For Those Who Wish to Dream: Emerging Theologians on Mission and Evangelism,* 2019, ISBN: 978-2-8254-1724-9

Risto Jukko and Jooseop Keum (Eds.), *Moving in the Spirit: Report of the WCC Conference on World Mission and Evangelism,* 2019, ISBN: 978-2-8254-1721-8

Risto Jukko (Ed.), *Moving in the Spirit: Report of the WCC Conference on World Mission and Evangelism,* Complete Digital Edition, 2019, ISBN: 978-2-8254-1722-5

Risto Jukko, Jooseop Keum and (Kay) Kyeong-Ah Woo (Eds.), *Called to Transforming Discipleship: Devotions from the WCC Conference on World Mission and Evangelism,* 2019, ISBN: 978-2-8254-1723-2

Come and See: A Theological Invitation to the Pilgrimage of Justice and Peace (Faith & Order Paper 224), 2019, ISBN: 978-2-8254-1725-6

Susan Durber and Fernando Enns (Eds.), *Walking Together: Reflections on the Ecumenical Pilgrimage of Justice and Peace,* Ebook edition, 2019, ISBN: 978-2-8254-1726-3

United and Uniting Churches: Two Messages (Faith and Order Paper 225), 2019, ISBN: 978-2-8254-1727-0

Pontifical Council for Interreligious Dialogue and the World Council of Churches, *Education for Peace in a Multi-Religious World: A Christian Perspective,* 2019, ISBN: 978-2-8254-1728-7

Moral Discernment in the Churches, Spanish edition, 2019, ISBN: 978-2-8254-1700-3

Moral Discernment in the Churches, German edition, 2019, ISBN: 978-2-8254-1729-4

Treatment Adherence and Faith Healing in the Context of HIV and AIDS in Africa (EHAIA), Kinwaranda Version, 2019, ISBN: 978-2-8254-1701-0

They Showed Us Unusual Kindness: Resources for the Week of Prayer for Christian Unity 2020 (F&O Paper 226), 2019, ISBN: 978-2-8254-1704-1

Minutes of the Faith and Order Commission Meeting (Nanjing, June 2019, Faith & Order Paper 227), 2019, ISBN: 978-2-8254-1705-8

Fulata Lusungu Moyo, *Healing Together: A Facilitator's Resource for Ecumenical Faith and Community Community-Based Counselling* (EHAIA), 2019, ISBN: 978-2-8254-1706-5

Jürgen Moltmann, *Hope in These Troubled Times,* 2019, ISBN: 978-2-8254-1713-3

Mwai Mokoka, *Health-Promoting Churches: Reflections on Health and Healing for Churches on Commemorative World Health Days,* 2020, ISBN: 978-2-8254-1708-9

Mwai Mokoka, *Health-Promoting Churches: Reflections on Health and Healing for Churches on Commemorative World Health Days,* Spanish edition, 2020, ISBN: 978-2-8254-1709-6

Ecumenical International Youth Day, 2020: Young People and Mental Health, 2020, ISBN: 978-2-8254-1730-0

Climate Justice with and for Children and Youth in Churches: Get Informed, Get Inspired, Take Action, 2020, ISBN: 978-2-8254-1731-7

The Light of Peace: The Churches and the Korean Peninsula, 2020, ISBN: 978-2-8254-1732-4

Healing the World: Bible Studies for the Pandemic Era, 2020, ISBN: 978-2-8254-1733-1

The Light of Peace: Churches in Solidarity with the Korean Peninsula, 2020, ISBN: 978-2-8254-1734-8

Pontifical Council for Interreligious Dialogue and the World Council of Churches, Serving a Wounded World in Interreligious Solidarity: A Christian call to reflection and action during COVID-19 and beyond, 2020, ISBN: 978-2-8254-1737-9

Globethics.net Publications

The list below is only a selection of our publications. To view the full collection, please visit our website.

All free products are provided free of charge and can be downloaded in PDF form from the Globethics.net library and at www.globethics.net/publications. Bulk print copies can be ordered from publications@globethics.net at special rates from the Global South.

Paid products not provided free of charge are indicated*.

The Director of the different Series of Globethics.net Publications

Prof. Dr. Obiora Ike, Executive Director of Globethics.net in Geneva and Professor of Ethics at the Godfrey Okoye University Enugu/Nigeria.

Contact for manuscripts and suggestions: publications@globethics.net

Global Series

Christoph Stückelberger, Walter Fust, Obiora Ike (eds.), *Global Ethics for Leadership. Values and Virtues for Life*, 2016, 444ppISBN: 978–2–88931–123–1

Dietrich Werner / Elisabeth Jeglitzka (eds.), *Eco-Theology, Climate Justice and Food Security: Theological Education and Christian Leadership Development*, 316pp. 2016, ISBN: 978–2–88931–145–3

Obiora Ike, Andrea Grieder and Ignace Haaz (Eds.), *Poetry and Ethics: Inventing Possibilities in Which We Are Moved to Action and How We Live Together*, 271pp. 2018, ISBN: 978–2–88931–242–9

Christoph Stückelberger / Pavan Duggal (Eds.), *Cyber Ethics 4.0: Serving Humanity with Values*, 503pp. 2018, ISBN: 978–2–88931–264–1

Texts Series

Ethics in the Information Society: The Nine 'P's. A Discussion Paper for the WSIS+10 Process 2013–2015, 2013, 32pp. ISBN: 978–2–940428–063–2

Principles on Equality and Inequality for a Sustainable Economy. Endorsed by the Global Ethics Forum 2014 with Results from Ben Africa Conference 2014, 2015, 41pp. ISBN: 978–2–88931–025–8

Water Ethics: Principles and Guidelines, 2019, 41pp. ISBN: 978–2–88931-313-6, available in three languages.

Theses Series

Sabina Kavutha Mutisya, *The Experience of Being a Divorced or Separated Single Mother: A Phenomenological Study*, 2019, 168pp. ISBN: 978-2-88931-274-0

Florence Muia, *Sustainable Peacebuilding Strategies. Sustainable Peacebuilding Operations in Nakuru County, Kenya: Contribution to the Catholic Justice and Peace Commission (CJPC)*, 2020, 195pp. ISBN: 978-2-88931-331-0

Mary Rose-Claret Ogbuehi, *The Struggle for Women Empowerment Through Education*, 2020, 410pp. ISBN: 978-2-88931-363-1

Focus Series

Maryann Ijeoma Egbujor, *The Relevance of Journalism Education in Kenya for Professional Identity and Ethical Standards*, 2018, 141pp. ISBN: 978–2–88931233–7

Christoph, Stückelberger, *Globalance. Ethics Handbook for a Balanced World Post-Covid*, 2020, 608pp. ISBN: 978-2-88931-368-6

Bosco Muchukiwa Rukakiza, *Résilience et transformation des conflits dans les États des Grands Lacs africains: Théorie, démarches et applications*, 2021, 126pp. ISBN: 978-2-88931-405-8

Praxis Series

Benoît Girardin / Evelyne Fiechter-Widemann (Eds.), *Éthique de l'eau: Pour un usage et une gestion justes et durables des ressources en eau*, 2020, 309pp. ISBN: 978-2-88931-337-2

Didier Ostermann, *Le rôle de l'Église maronite dans la construction du Liban:1500 ans d'histoire, du Ve au XXe siècle*, 2020, 142pp. ISBN: 978-2-88931-365-5

African Law Series

Pascal Mukonde Musulay, *Démocratie électorale en Afrique subsahar-ienne*, 2016, 209pp. ISBN: 978–2–88931–156–9

Pascal Mukonde Musulay, *Droits, libertés et devoirs de la personne et des peuples en droit international africain Tome I Promotion et protection,* 282pp. 2021, ISBN: 978-2-88931-397-6

Pascal Mukonde Musulay, *Droits, libertés et devoirs de la personne et des peuples en droit international africain Tome II Libertés, droits et obligations démocratiques,* 332pp. 2021, ISBN: 978-2-88931-399-0

Ambroise Katambu Bulambo, *Règlement judiciaire des conflits électoraux. Précis de droit comparé africain,* 2021, 672pp., ISBN 978-2-88931-403-4

Osita C. Eze, *Africa Charter on Rights & Duties, Enforcement Mechanism,* 2021, 406pp, ISBN: 978-2-88931-414-0

Agape Series

崔万田 Cui Wantian, *爱+经济学 Agape Economics,* 2020, 420pp. ISBN: 978-2-88931-349-5

Cui Wantian, Christoph Stückelberger, *The Better Sinner: A Practical Guide on Corruption, 2020,* 37pp. ISBN: 978-2-88931-339-6 (Available also in Chinese).

Anh Tho Andres Kammler, *FaithInvest: Impactful Cooperation. Report of the International Conference Geneva 2020,* 2020, 70pp. ISBN: 978-2-88931-357-0

崔万田 Cui Wantian, 价值观创造价值　企业家信仰于企业绩效 *Values Create Value. Impact through Faith-based Entrepreneurship,* 2020, 432pp. IBSN: 978-2-88931-361-7

Moses C. 编辑, 圣商灵粮：中国基督徒企业家的灵修日记 *Daily Bread for Christians in Business: The Spiritual Diary of Chinese Christian Entrepre-neurs,* 412pp. 2021, ISBN: 978-2-88931-391-4

Haicun Kong, *Walk the Talk. Africa / Asia Focus. Report of the International Online Conference, Jan / Mar 2021,* 2021, 41pp. ISBN: 978-2-88931- 411-9

China Christian Series

Spirituality 4.0 at the Workplace and FaithInvest - Building Bridges, 2019, 107pp. ISBN: 978-2-88931-304-4

海茵兹·吕格尔 / 克里斯多夫·芝格里斯特 (Christoph Sigrist/ Heinz Rüegger) *Diaconia: An Introduction. Theological Foundation of Christian Service,* 2019, 433pp. ISBN: 978-2-88931-302-0

Education Ethics Series

Divya Singh / Christoph Stückelberger (Eds.), *Ethics in Higher Education Values-driven Leaders for the Future,* 2017, 367pp. ISBN: 978–2–88931–165–1

Obiora Ike / Chidiebere Onyia (Eds.), *Ethics in Higher Education, Foundation for Sustainable Development,* 2018, 645pp. ISBN: 978-2-88931-217-7

Obiora Ike / Chidiebere Onyia (Eds.), *Ethics in Higher Education, Religions and Traditions in Nigeria* 2018, 198pp. ISBN: 978-2-88931-219-1

Obiora F. Ike, Justus Mbae, Chidiebere Onyia (Eds.), *Mainstreaming Ethics in Higher Education: Research Ethics in Administration, Finance, Education, Environment and Law Vol. 1,* 2019, 779pp. ISBN: 978-2-88931-300-6

Ikechukwu J. Ani/Obiora F. Ike (Eds.), *Higher Education in Crisis Sustaining Quality Assurance and Innovation in Research through Applied Ethics,* 2019, 214pp. ISBN: 978-2-88931-323-5

Deivit Montealegre / María Eugenia Barroso (Eds.), *Ethics in Higher Educa-tion, a Transversal Dimension: Challenges for Latin America. Ética en educa-ción superior, una dimensión transversal: Desafíos para América Latina,* 2020, 148pp. ISBN: 978-2-88931-359-4

Obiora Ike, Justus Mbae, Chidiebere Onyia, Herbert Makinda (Eds.), *Mainstreaming Ethics in Higher Education Vol. 2,* 2021, 420pp. ISBN: 978-2-88931-383-9

Christoph Stückelberger/ Joseph Galgalo/ Samuel Kobia (Eds.), *Leadership with Integrity. Higher Education from Vocation to Funding,* 2021, 288pp. ISBN: 978-2-88931-389-1

Copublications & Other

Obiora F. Ike, *Moral and Ethical Leadership, Human Rights and Conflict Resolution – African and Global Contexts*, 2020, 191pp. ISBN: 978-2-88931-333-4

Kenneth R. Ross, *Mission Rediscovered: Transforming Disciples*, 2020, 138pp. ISBN: 978-2-88931-369-3

Obiora Ike, Amélé Adamavi-Aho Ekué, Anja Andriamay, Lucy Howe López (Eds.), *Who Cares About Ethics?* 2020, 352pp. ISBN: 978-2-88931-381-5

This is only selection of our latest publications, to view our full collection please visit:

www.globethics.net/publications